ROUGH GUIDES PHRASEBOOK

GERMAN

ROUGH
GUIDES

Contacting the Editors

Every effort has been made to provide accurate information in this publication, but changes are inevitable. The publisher cannot be responsible for any resulting loss, inconvenience or injury.
We would appreciate it if readers would call our attention to any errors or outdated information. We also welcome your suggestions; if you come across a relevant expression not in our phrase book, please contact us at:**mail@uk.roughguides.com**

All Rights Reserved
© 2019 APA Publications (UK) Ltd.

Cover & Interior Design: Slawomir Krajewski
Head of Production: Rebeka Davies
Production Manager: Rebecca Hancock
Picture Researcher: Slawomir Krajewski
Cover Photo: all shutterstock

Interior Photos: all shutterstock

CONTENTS

INTRODUCTION

PRACTICALITIES

ON THE WAY

FOOD

PEOPLE

DICTIONARY

PRONUNCIATION

This section is designed to make you familiar with the sounds of German, using our simplified phonetic transcription. You'll find the pronunciation of the German letters explained below, together with their 'imitated' equivalents. This system is used throughout the phrase book; simply read the pronunciation as if it were English, noting any special rules below.

The German alphabet is the same as English, with the addition of the letter **ß**. Some vowels appear with an **Umlaut: ä**, **ü** and **ö**. Of note, German recently underwent a spelling reform. The letter **ß** is now shown as **ss** after a short vowel, but is unchanged after a long vowel or diphthong. In print and dated material, you may still see the **ß**; e.g., formerly **Kuß**, now **Kuss**.

Stress has been indicated in the phonetic transcription: the underlined letters should be pronounced with more stress, e.g., *Adresse*, *ah-drehs-uh*.

CONSONANTS

Letter	Approximate Pronunciation	Symbol	Example	Pronunciation
b	1. at the end of a word or between a vowel and a consonant, like p in up	p	**ab**	*ahp*
	2. elsewhere, as in English	b	**bis**	*bihs*
c	1. before e, i, ä and ö, like ts in hits	ts	**Celsius**	*tsehl•see•oos*
	2. elsewhere, like c in cats	k	**Café**	*kah•feh*
ch	1. like k in kit	k	**Wachs**	*vahks*
	2. after vowels, like ch in Scottish loch	kh	**doch**	*dohkh*

Letter	Approximate Pronunciation	Symbol	Example	Pronunciation
d	1. at the end of the word or before a consonant, like t in eat	t	**Rad**	*raht*
	2. elsewhere, like d in do	d	**danke**	*dahn • kuh*
g	1. at the end of a word, sounds like k	k	**fertig**	*fehr • teek*
	2. like g in go	g	**gehen**	*geh • uhn*
j	like y in yes	y	**ja**	*yah*
qu	like k + v in onion	kv	**Quark**	*kvahrk*
r	pronounced in the back of the mouth	r	**warum**	*vah • room*
s	1. before or vowels, like z in zoo	z	**sie**	*zee*
	2. before p and t, like sh in shut	sh	**Sport**	*shpohrt*
	3. elsewhere, like s in sit	s	**es ist**	*ehs ihst*
ß	like s in sit	s	**groß**	*grohs*
sch	like sh in shut	sh	**schnell**	*shnehl*
tsch	like ch in chip	ch	**deutsch**	*doych*
tz	lke ts in hits	ch	**Platz**	*plahts*
v	1. like f in for	f	**vier**	*feer*
	2. in foreign words, like v i voice	v	**Vase**	*vah • seh*
w	like v in voice	v	**wie**	*vee*
z	like ts in hits	ts	**zeigen**	*tsie • gehn*

Letters f, h, k, l, m, n, p, t and x are pronounced as in English.

VOWELS

Letter	Approximate Pronunciation	Symbol	Example	Pronunciation
a	like a in father	ah	**Tag**	*tahk*
ä	1. like e in let	eh	**Lärm**	*lehrm*
	2. like a in late	ay	**spät**	*shpayt*
e	1. like e in let	eh	**schnell**	*shnehl*
	2. at the end of a word, if the syllable is not stressed, like u in us	uh	**bitte**	<u>*biht*</u> • *tuh*
i	1. like i in hit, before a doubled consonant	ih	**billig**	*bih* • *leek*
	2. otherwise, like ee in meet	ee	**ihm**	*eem*
o	like o in home	oh	**voll**	*fohl*
ö	like o in fern	er	**schön**	*shern*
u	like oo in boot	oo	**Nuss**	*noos*
ü	like ew in new	er	**über**	<u>*ew*</u> • *behr*
y	like ew in new	ew	**typisch**	<u>*tew*</u> • *peesh*

COMBINED VOWELS

Letter	Approximate Pronunciation	Symbol	Example	Pronunciation
ai, ay ei, ey	like ie in tie	ie	**nein**	*nien*
ao, au	like ow in now	ow	**auf**	*owf*
äu, eu	like oy in boy oy	oy	**neu**	*noy*

HOW TO USE THE APP

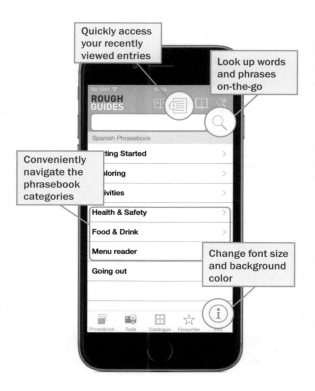

Quickly access your recently viewed entries

Look up words and phrases on-the-go

Conveniently navigate the phrasebook categories

Change font size and background color

No SIM
17:55

ROUGH GUIDES

Spanish Phrasebook

tting Started >

ploring >

ivities >

Health & Safety >

Food & Drink >

Menu reader

Going out

Phrasebook   Tools   Catalogue   Favourites   Info

Save the most useful everyday words and phrases to your Favorites

Use the Flash Cards Quiz to learn and memorize new words easily

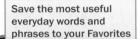

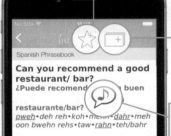

Spanish Phrasebook

Can you recommend a good restaurant/ bar?
¿Puede recomend⸱⸱⸱⸱ buen

restaurante/bar?
*pweh•deh reh•koh•mehn•dahr•meh
oon bwehn rehs•taw•rahn•teh/bahr*

Take all digital advantages of the app: listen to words and phrases pronounced by native speakers

Is there a t...

Phrasebook Tools Catalogue Favourites Info

To learn how to Activate the app, see the inside back cover of this phrasebook.

GRAMMAR

REGULAR VERBS

Regular verbs in German are conjugated as in the table below. Note that the past is expressed with **haben** (to have) or **sein** (to be) plus the past participle. The future is formed with **werden** (will) plus the infinitive.

BEZAHLEN	FDH	PRESENT	PAST	FUTURE
I	ich	bezahle	habe bezahlt	*werde bezahlen*
you (inf.)	du	bezahlst	hast bezahlt	*wirst bezahlen*
he/she/it	er/sie/es	bezahlt	hat bezahlt	*wird bezahlen*
we	wir	bezahlen	haben bezahlt	*werden bezahlen*
you (pl.) (inf.)	ihr	bezahlt	habt bezahlt	*werdet bezahlen*
they/you	sie/Sie	bezahlen	haben bezahlt	*werden bezahlen*

Example: **Ich bezahle bar.** I'll pay in cash.
Er m /sie f bezahlt mit Kreditkarte. He/She will pay with credit card.

MACHEN	FDH	PRESENT	PAST	FUTURE
I	ich	**mache**	**habe gemacht**	*werde machen*
you (inf.)	du	**machst**	**hast gemacht**	**wirst machen**
he/she/it	er/sie/es	**macht**	**hat gemacht**	*wird machen*
we	wir	**machen**	**haben gemacht**	*werden machen*
you (pl.) (inf.)	ihr	**macht**	**habt gemacht**	*werdet machen*
they/you	sie/Sie	**machen**	**haben gemacht**	*werden machen*

Examples: **Ich mache hier Urlaub.** I'm here on vacation.
Was machen Sie beruflich? What do you do (for work)?

IRREGULAR VERBS

There are a number of irregular verbs in German. Two common irregular verbs in German are **haben** (to have) and **sein** (to be). Conjugations follow:

HABEN	FDH	PRESENT	PAST	FUTURE
I	ich	**habe**	**habe gehabt**	*werde haben*
you (inf.)	du	**hast**	**hast gehabt**	*wirst haben*
he/she/it	er/sie/es	**hat**	**hat gehabt**	*wird haben*
we	wir	**haben**	**haben gehabt**	*werden haben*
you (pl.) (inf.)	ihr	**habt**	**habt gehabt**	*werdet haben*
they/you	sie/Sie	**haben**	**haben gehabt**	*werden haben*

Example: **Ich habe einen Koffer.** I have one suitcase.
Ihr habt viel zu tun. You guys have a lot to do.

SEIN	FDH	PRESENT	PAST	FUTURE
I	ich	bin	bin gewesen	*werde sein*
you (inf.)	du	bist	bist gewesen	*wirst sein*
he/she/it	er/sie/es	ist	ist gewesen	*wird sein*
we	wir	sind	sind gewesen	*werden sein*
you (pl.) (inf.)	ihr	seid	seid gewesen	*werdet sein*
they/you	sie/Sie	sind	sind gewesen	*werden sein*

Example: **Ich bin geschäftlich hier.** I am here on business.
Wir sind glücklich. We are happy.

WORD ORDER

German is similar to English in terms of word order for simple sentences; it follows the subject-verb-object pattern.
Example: **Wir lassen unser Gepäck hier.** We leave our luggage here.
When the sentence doesn't begin with a subject, the word order changes: the verb and the subject are inverted.
Examples:

	Er	ist	in Berlin.		He is in Berlin.
Heute	ist	er	in Berlin.		Today he is in Berlin.
	Wir	sind	in Berlin	gewesen.	We were in Berlin.

To ask a question, begin with the verb and follow with the subject, as in English. Example: **Seid ihr in Köln gewesen?** Have you been to Cologne? (Literally: Have you to Cologne been?)

NEGATION

The negative is formed in German by putting **nicht** after the verb.

Example: **Ich bin Thomas**. I am Thomas.
Ich bin nicht Thomas. I am not Thomas.

If a noun is used, the negation is made by adding **kein** (masculine and neuter), or **keine** (feminine). For plural nouns, always add **keine**.

Example: **Wir haben keine Einzelzimmer.**
We don't have any single rooms.

IMPERATIVES

Whereas in English the imperative always looks like the infinitive ('Go!'), in German it is derived from the **du-/Sie-** form of the present tense. In the **du-** form, the -st is dropped.

All other forms are identical to the present tense. Note that the verb always comes first in commands.

		Go!
du	you (inf.)	**Geh!**
ihr	you (pl.) (inf.)	**Geht!**
Sie	you	**Gehen Sie!**
wir	we	**Gehen wir!** (Let's go!)

NOUNS & ARTICLES

In German, all nouns are capitalized. German nouns are also gender-specific; they can be masculine, feminine or neuter. There is no easy way to determine whether a noun is masculine, feminine or neuter.

There are three definite articles (the) in German: **der**, **die** and **das**. Masculine words use **der**, feminine words use **die** and neuter words use **das**.

The only way to tell whether a word is masculine, feminine or neuter is to look at the article. For this reason, it is best to memorize the article when learning the word. For plural nouns using a definite article, all genders use **die**.

Definite examples: **der Mann** (the man), **die Männer** (the men); **die Frau** (the woman), **die Frauen** (the women); **das Kind** (neuter) (the child), **die Kinder** (neuter) (the children)
There are four cases in German. The definite articles are as follows:

	Masculine	Feminine	Neuter	Plural (all genders)
nominative	der	die	das	die
accusative	den	die	das	die
dative	dem	der	dem	den
genitive	des	der	des	der

German uses two indefinite articles (a/an): **ein** and **eine**. Masculine and neuter nouns use **ein**, and feminine nouns use **eine**.

For plural nouns, the indefinite article is dropped, as in English. Indefinite examples include: **ein Zug** (a train), **Züge** (trains); **eine Karte** (a map), **Karten** (maps)

ADJECTIVES

Adjectives must agree with the nouns they modify. Adjective endings change based on the article used and the case.
For masculine nouns, **−er** is added to the adjective after an indefinite article and **−e** is added after a definite article.
Example: **ein kleiner Herr** a short gentleman
der kleine Herr the short gentleman
For feminine nouns, **−e** is added to the adjective after both an indefinite and a definite article.
Example: **eine kluge Frau** an intelligent woman
die kluge Frau the intelligent woman
For neuter nouns, **−es** is added to the adjective after an indefinite article, while **−e** is added to the adjective after a definite article.
Example: **ein großes Land** a big country
das große Land the big country

COMPARATIVES & SUPERLATIVES

In German, the comparative of an adjective is usually formed by adding **−er** to the end of the adjective.
Examples: **klein** (small), **kleiner** (smaller); **billig** (cheap), **billiger** (cheaper); **groß** (big), **größer** (bigger)
The superlative is formed by adding **−sten** or **−esten** to the end of the adjective. If the adjective has a vowel of **a**, **o** or **u**, it may change to **ä**, **ö** or **ü** in the comparative and superlative forms.
Examples: **klein** (small), **kleinsten** (smallest); **billig** (cheap), **billigsten** (cheapest); **groß** (big); **größten** (biggest)

POSSESSIVE ADJECTIVES

Possessive adjectives must agree in gender and number with the noun they are associated with.

| | Singular | | Plural |
	Masculine/ Neuter	Feminine	
my	mein	meine	meine
your (inf.)	dein	deine	deine
his/its	sein	seine	seine
her/their	ihr	ihre	ihre
your (pl.) (inf.)	Ihr	Ihre	Ihre
our	unser	unsere	unsere

Example: **Wir lassen unser Gepäck im Hotel.** We leave our luggage in the hotel.

POSSESSIVE PRONOUNS

Possessive pronouns agree in gender and number with the noun they replace.

	Masculine	Feminine	Neuter
mine	meiner	meine	meines
yours (inf.)	deiner	deine	deines
his/its	seiner	seine	seines
hers/theirs	ihrer	ihre	ihres
ours	unserer	unsere	unseres
yours (pl.) (inf.)	eurer	eure	eures

Example: **Wem gehört der Schlüssel?** Whose key is this? **Das ist meiner.** It's mine.

ADVERBS & ADVERBIAL EXPRESSIONS

In German, adverbs are usually identical to adjectives but, unlike adjectives, their endings don't change.
Examples:
Adjective: **das gute Essen** the good food
Adverb: **Sie sprechen gut Deutsch.** You speak German well.

PRACTICALITIES

THE BASICS

NUMBERS

NEED TO KNOW

0	**null**	*nool*
1	**eins**	*iens*
2	**zwei**	*tsvie*
3	**drei**	*drie*
4	**vier**	*feer*
5	**fünf**	*fewnf*
6	**sechs**	*zehks*
7	**sieben**	*zeeb•uhn*
8	**acht**	*ahkht*
9	**neun**	*noyn*
10	**zehn**	*tsehn*
11	**elf**	*ehlf*
12	**zwölf**	*tsverlf*

13	**dreizehn**	_driet • sehn_
14	**vierzehn**	_feert • sehn_
15	**fünfzehn**	_fewnf • tsehn_
16	**sechszehn**	_zehk • tsehn_
17	**siebzehn**	_zeep • tsehn_
18	**achtzehn**	_ahkht • tsehn_
19	**neunzehn**	_noyn • tsehn_
20	**zwanzig**	_tsvahnt • seek_
21	**einundzwanzig**	_ien • oond • tsvahn • tseek_
22	**zweiundzwanzig**	_tsvie • oond • tsvahn • tseek_
30	**dreißig**	_drie • seekh_
31	**einunddreißig**	_ien • oont • drie • seekh_
40	**vierzig**	_feert • seek_
50	**fünfzig**	_fewnf • tseeg_
60	**sechzig**	_zehkht • seeg_
70	**siebzig**	_zeeb • tseeg_

80	**achtzig**
	ahkht • tseeg
90	**neunzig**
	noynt • seek
100	**einhundert**
	ien • hoon • dehrt
101	**einhunderteins**
	ien • hoon • dehr • tiens
200	**zweihundert**
	tsvie • hoon • dehrt
500	**fünfhundert**
	fewnf • hoon • dehrt
1,000	**eintausend**
	ien • tow • zuhnt
10,000	**zehntausend**
	tsehn • tow • zuhnt
1,000,000	**eine Million**
	ien • uh mihl • _yohn_

ORDINAL NUMBERS

first	**erste**
	ehrs • tuh
second	**zweite**
	tsviet • uh
third	**dritte**
	driht • tuh
fourth	**vierte**
	feer • tuh
fifth	**fünfte**
	fewnf • tuh

once	**einmal**
	ien • mahl
twice	**zweimal**
	tsvie • mahl
three times	**dreimal**
	drie • mahl

TIME

NEED TO KNOW

What time is it?	**Wie spät ist es?**	
	vee shpayt ihst ehs	
It's midday.	**Es ist zwölf.**	
	ehs ihst tsverlf	
At midnight.	**Um Mitternacht.**	
	oom miht • tehr • nahkht	
From one o'clock	**Von eins bis zwei.**	
to two o'clock.	*fohn iens bihs tsvie*	
Five past three.	**Fünf nach drei.**	
	fewnf nahkh drie	
A quarter to four.	**Viertel vor vier.**	
	feert • uhl fohr feer	
5:30 a.m./5:30 p.m.	**Fünf Uhr dreißig/Siebzehn Uhr dreißig**	
	fewnf oohr drie • seeg/zeeb • tsuhn oohr drie • seeg	

Germans use the 24-hour clock in formal contexts (radio, TV, transportation schedules and digital clocks) or when confusion might otherwise arise. The morning hours from 1:00 a.m. to noon are the same as in English. After that, just add 12: so 1:00 p.m. would be 13:00, 5:00 p.m. would be 17:00 and so on. This system eliminates the necessity of 'a.m.' and 'p.m.' markers. When the 12-hour clock is used, **morgens** (in the morning) and **abends** (in the evening) are added after the number for clarity.

DAYS

NEED TO KNOW

Monday	**Montag**	
	mohn • tahk	
Tuesday	**Dienstag**	
	deens • tahk	
Wednesday	**Mittwoch**	
	miht • vohkh	
Thursday	**Donnerstag**	
	dohn • ehrs • tahk	
Friday	**Freitag**	
	frie • tahk	
Saturday	**Samstag**	
	zahms • tahk	
Sunday	**Sonntag**	
	zohn • tahk	

DATES

yesterday	**gestern** _gehs_ • tehrn
today	**heute** _hoy_ • tuh
tomorrow	**morgen** _mohr_ • guhn
day	**Tag** tahk
week	**Woche** _vohkh_ • uh
month	**Monat** _moh_ • naht
year	**Jahr** yahr

German calendars and weeks, like the U.K., are arranged Monday through Sunday (in contrast to the U.S., where calendars run Sunday through Saturday).

MONTHS

January	**Januar** _yahn_ • wahr
February	**Februar** _fehb_ • rooahr
March	**März** mehrts
April	**April** ah • _prihl_

May	**Mai**
	mie
June	**Juni**
	yoo • nee
July	**Juli**
	yoo • lee
August	**August**
	ow • goost
September	**September**
	zehp • tehm • behr
October	**Oktober**
	ohk • toh • behr
November	**November**
	noh • vehm • behr
December	**Dezember**
	deh • tsehm • behr

SEASONS

in...	**im ...**
	ihm ...
spring	**Frühling**
	frewh • leeng
summer	**Sommer**
	zohm • ehr
fall [autumn]	**Herbst**
	hehrbst
winter	**Winter**
	vihnt • ehr

HOLIDAYS

January 1: New Year's Day, **Neujahrstag**
January 6: Epiphany, **Heilige Drei Könige**
May 1: Labor Day, **Tag der Arbeit**
August 15: Assumption Day, **Mariä Himmelfahrt**
October 3: German Unity Day, **Tag der Deutschen Einheit**
November 1: All Saint's Day, **Allerheiligen**
December 25: Christmas, **Erster Weihnachtstag**
December 26: St. Stephen's Day [Boxing Day], **Zweiter Weihnachtstag**
The Easter (movable) holidays are:
Ascension Day, **Christ Himmelfahrt**
Easter Sunday, **Ostersonntag**
Easter Monday, **Ostermontag**
Feast of Corpus Christi, **Fronleichnam**
Good Friday, **Karfreitag**
Pentecost, **Pfinstsonntag**
Pentecost Monday, **Pfinstmontag**

One of Germany's most famous festivals is **Oktoberfest**, held each September in Munich. This food and beer festival extends for more than two weeks and is attended by about six million visitors from around the world. Another popular festival is **Karneval**, celebrated with parades and parties the week before Lent in areas that have substantial Catholic populations. Christmas festivities and markets are also very popular in Germany. Locals and tourists alike visit these markets to purchase local handmade crafts such as toys, wooden carvings, marionettes, candles, lambskin shoes and much more. There are plenty of food vendors available with numerous tasty treats to try.

ARRIVAL & DEPARTURE

NEED TO KNOW

I'm on vacation [holiday].	**Ich mache Urlaub.** *eekh <u>mahkh</u> • uh <u>oor</u> • lowb*
I'm on business.	**Ich bin auf Geschäftsreise.** *eekh bihn owf guh • <u>shehfts</u> • rie • zuh*
I'm going to…	**Ich reise nach …** *eekh <u>rie</u> • zuh nahkh …*
I'm staying at the…Hotel.	**Ich übernachte im Hotel …** *eekh ew • buhr • <u>nahkh</u> • tuh ihm hoh • <u>tehl</u> …*

YOU MAY HEAR…

Ihren Reisepass, bitte. *eer • uhn <u>rie</u> • zuh • pahs <u>biht</u> • tuh*	Your passport, please.
Was ist der Grund Ihrer Reise? *vahs ihst dehr groont <u>ihr</u> • uhr <u>rie</u> • zuh*	What's the purpose of your visit?
Wo übernachten Sie? *voh ew • behr • <u>nahkh</u> • tuhn zee*	Where are you staying?
Wie lange bleiben Sie? *vee <u>lahng</u> • uh <u>blie</u> • buhn zee*	How long are you staying?
Mit wem reisen Sie? *miht vehm rie • zuhn zee*	Who are you traveling with?

BORDER CONTROL

I'm just passing through.	**Ich bin auf der Durchreise.** *eekh been owf dehr <u>doorkh</u> • rie • zuh*
I'd like to declare…	**Ich möchte … verzollen.** *eekh <u>merkh</u> • tuh … fehr • <u>tsoh</u> • luhn*
I have nothing to declare.	**Ich habe nichts zu verzollen.** *eekh <u>hah</u> • buh neekhts tsoo fehr • <u>tsoh</u> • luhn*

YOU MAY HEAR…

Haben Sie etwas zu verzollen? *<u>hah</u> • buhn zee <u>eht</u> • vahs tsoo fehr • <u>tsoh</u> • luhn*	Do you have anything to declare?
Darauf müssen Sie Zoll zahlen. *dahr • <u>owf</u> <u>mew</u> • suhn zee tsol <u>tsah</u> • luhn*	You must pay duty on this.
Öffnen Sie diese Tasche. *<u>erf</u> • nuhn zee <u>dee</u> • zuh <u>tah</u> • shuh*	Open this bag.

YOU MAY SEE…

ZOLL	customs
ZOLLFREIE WAREN	duty-free goods
ZOLLPFLICHTIGE WAREN	goods to declare
NICHTS ZU VERZOLLEN	nothing to declare
PASSKONTROLLE	passport control
POLIZEI	police

MONEY

NEED TO KNOW

Where's…?	**Wo ist …?**
	voh ihst …
the ATM	**der Bankautomat**
	dehr bahnk • ow • toh • maht
the bank	**die Bank**
	dee bahnk
the currency exchange office	**die Wechselstube**
	dee vehkh • zuhl • shtoo • buh
When does the bank open/close?	**Wann öffnet/schließt die Bank?**
	vahn erf • nuht/shleest dee bahnk
I'd like to change dollars/pounds into euros.	**Ich möchte Dollar/Pfund in Euro wechseln.**
	eekh mehrkh • tuh doh • lahr/pfoont ihn oy • roh vehkh • zuhln
I'd like to cash traveler's checks [cheques].	**Ich möchte Reiseschecks einlösen.**
	eekh mehrkh • tuh rie • zuh • shehks ien • ler • zuhn

AT THE BANK

I'd like to change money/get a cash advance.	**Ich möchte Geld wechseln.**
	eekh mehrkh • tuh gehlt vehkh • zuhln
What's the exchange rate/fee?	**Was ist der Wechselkurs/die Gebühr?**
	vahs ihst dehr vehkh • zuhl • koors/dee guh • bewr
I think there's a mistake.	**Ich glaube, hier stimmt etwas nicht.**
	eekh glow • buh heer shtihmt eht • vahs neekht

I lost my traveler's cheques.	**Ich habe meine Reiseschecks verloren.** *eekh <u>hah</u> • buh <u>mie</u> • nuh <u>rie</u> • zuh • shecks fehr • <u>loh</u> • ruhn*
My card was stolen/doesn't work.	**Meine Karte wurde gestohlen/ funktioniert nicht.** *<u>mie</u> • nuh <u>kahr</u> • tuh <u>voor</u> • duh guh • <u>shtoh</u> • luhn/foonk • tzyoh • <u>neert</u> neekht*
My card was lost.	**Ich habe meine Karte verloren.** *eek <u>hah</u> • buh <u>mie</u> • nuh <u>kahr</u> • tuh fehr • <u>loh</u> • ruhn*
The ATM ate my card.	**Der Bankautomat hat meine Karte eingezogen.** *dehr <u>bahnk</u> • ow • toh • maht haht <u>mie</u> • nuh <u>kahr</u> • tuh <u>ien</u> • geh • tsoh • ghun*

YOU MAY SEE...

KARTE HIER EINFÜHREN	insert card here
ABBRECHEN	cancel
LÖSCHEN	clear
EINGEBEN	enter
PIN-NUMMER	PIN
ABHEBUNG	withdrawal
VOM GIROKONTO	from checking [current] account
VOM SPARKONTO	from savings account
QUITTUNG	receipt

The best rates for exchanging money will be found at banks. You can also change money at travel agencies, currency exchange offices and hotels, though the rate may not be as good. Traveler's checks are accepted at most banks (though banks are not required to accept them) and currency exchange offices, but a variable fee will be charged. Cash can be obtained from **Bankautomaten** (ATMs) with many international bank and credit cards. ATMs are multilingual, so English-language instructions can be selected. Remember to bring your passport when you want to change money.

YOU MAY SEE...

German currency is the **Euro €**, divided into 100 **Cent**.
Coins: 1, 2, 5, 10, 20, 50 **Cent**; €1, 2
Notes: **€**5, 10, 20, 50, 100, 200, 500

CONVERSATION

NEED TO KNOW

Hello!	**Hallo!**
	hah • loh
How are you?	**Wie geht es Ihnen?**
	vee geht ehs eehn • uhn
Fine, thanks.	**Gut, danke.**
	goot dahn • kuh
Excuse me!	**Entschuldigung!**
	ehnt • shool • dee • goong
Do you speak English?	**Sprechen Sie Englisch?**
	shpreh • khuhn zee ehn • gleesh
What's your name?	**Wie heißen Sie?**
	vee hie • suhn zee
My name is...	**Mein Name ist ...**
	mien nahm • uh ihst ...
Nice to meet you.	**Schön, Sie kennenzulernen.**
	shern zeekeh • nehn • tsoo • lehr • nehn
Where are you from?	**Woher kommen Sie?**
	voh • hehr koh • muhn zee
I'm from the U.S./ U.K.	**Ich komme aus den USA/ Großbritannien.**
	eekh koh • muh ows dehn oo • ehs • ah/ grohs • bree • tah • nee • ehn
What do you do for a living?	**Was machen Sie beruflich?**
	vahs mah • khuhn zee beh • roof • likh
I work for...	**Ich arbeite für ...**
	eekh ahr • bie • tuh fewr ...
I'm a student.	**Ich bin Student.**
	eekh bihn shtoo • dehnt

I'm retired.	**Ich bin Rentner.**
	eekh been <u>rehnt</u> • nehr
Do you like…?	**Mögen Sie …?**
	<u>mer</u> • guhn zee …
Goodbye.	**Auf Wiedersehen.**
	owf <u>vee</u> • dehr • zehn
See you later.	**Bis bald.**
	bihs bahld

When addressing anyone but a very close friend, it is polite to use a title: **Herr** (Mr.), **Frau** (Miss/Ms./Mrs.) or **Herr Dr.** (Dr.), and to speak to him or her using **Sie**, the formal form of 'you', until you are asked to use the familiar **Du**.

LANGUAGE DIFFICULTIES

Do you speak English?	**Sprechen Sie Englisch?**
	shpreh • khehn zee <u>ehn</u> • gleesh
Does anyone here speak English?	**Spricht hier jemand Englisch?**
	shpreekht heer <u>yeh</u> • mahnt <u>ehn</u> • gleesh
I don't speak (much) German.	**Ich spreche kein (nicht viel) Deutsch.**
	eekh <u>shpreh</u> • khuh kien (neekht feel) doych
Can you speak more slowly, please?	**Können Sie bitte langsamer sprechen?**
	<u>ker</u> • nuhn zee biht • tuh <u>lahng</u> • sahm • ehr <u>shpreh</u> • khuhn
Can you repeat that, please?	**Können Sie das bitte wiederholen?**
	<u>ker</u> • nuhn zee dahs <u>biht</u> • tuh vee • dehr • <u>hoh</u> • luhn
Excuse me?	**Wie bitte?**
	vee <u>biht</u> • tuh

What was that?	**Was haben Sie gesagt?**
	vahs hah • buhn zee guh • zahgt
Can you spell it?	**Können Sie das buchstabieren?**
	ker • nuhn zee dahs book • shtah • bee • ruhn
Write it down, please.	**Bitte schreiben Sie es auf.**
	biht • tuh shrie • buhn zee ehs owf
Can you translate this into English for me?	**Können Sie das für mich ins Englische übersetzen?**
	ker • nuhn zee dahs fewr meekh ihns ehn • glee • shuh ew • behr • zeh • tsuhn
What does… mean?	**Was bedeutet …?**
	vahs beh • doyt • eht …
I understand.	**Ich verstehe.**
	eekh fehr • shteh • uh
I don't understand.	**Ich verstehe nicht.**
	eekh fehr • shteh • uh neekht
Do you understand?	**Verstehen Sie?**
	fehr • shteh • uhn zee

YOU MAY HEAR…

Ich spreche nur wenig Englisch.
eekh shpreh • khuh noor veh • neek ehn • gleesh

I only speak a little English.

Ich spreche kein Englisch.
eekh shpreh • khuh kien ehn • gleesh

I don't speak English.

MAKING FRIENDS

Hello!	**Hallo!**
	hah • loh
Good morning.	**Guten Morgen.**
	goo • tuhn mohr • guhn
Good afternoon.	**Guten Tag.**
	goo • tuhn tahk
Good evening.	**Guten Abend.**
	goo • tuhn ah • behnt
My name is…	**Mein Name ist …**
	mien nahm • uh ihst …
What's your name?	**Wie heißen Sie?**
	vee hie • sehn zee
I'd like to introduce you to…	**Ich möchte Sie gern … vorstellen.**
	eekh merkh • tuh zee gehrn … fohr • shteh • luhn
Pleased to meet you.	**Angenehm.**
	ahn • guh • nehm
How are you?	**Wie geht es Ihnen?**
	vee geht ehs eehn • uhn
Fine, thanks. And you?	**Gut, danke. Und Ihnen?**
	goot dahn • kuh oont eehn • uhn

In Germany, it's polite to shake hands, both when you meet and say goodbye. Relatives and close friends may hug or kiss cheeks.

TRAVEL TALK

I'm here on business.	**Ich bin geschäftlich hier.** *eekh bihn guh • shehft • leekh heer*
I'm here on vacation.	**Ich mache hier Urlaub.** *eekh mahk • uh heer oor • lowb*
I'm studying here.	**Ich bin zum Studieren hier.** *eekh bihn tsoom shtoo • dee • ruhn heer*
I'm staying for…	**Ich bleibe …** *eekh blie • buh …*
I've been here…	**Ich bin seit … hier.** *eekh been ziet … heer*
a day	**einem Tag** *ien • uhm tahk*
a week	**einer Woche** *ien • uhr voh • khuh*
a month	**einem Monat** *ien • uhm moh • naht*
Where are you from?	**Woher kommen Sie?** *voh • hehr koh • muhn zee*
I'm from…	**Ich komme aus …** *eekh koh • muh ows …*

For Numbers, see page 22.

PERSONAL

Who are you with?	**Mit wem sind Sie hier?** *miht vehm zihnt zee heer*
I'm here alone.	**Ich bin allein hier.** *eekh bihn ah • lien heer*
How old are you?	**Wie alt sind Sie?** *vee ahlt zihnt zee*

I'm…	**Ich bin …**
	eekh bihn …
I'm with…	**Ich bin mit … hier.**
	eekh been miht … heer
my husband/wife	**meinem Mann/meiner Frau**
	mie • nuhm mahn/mie • nuhr frow
my boyfriend/	**meinem Freund/meiner Freundin**
my girlfriend	*mie • nuhm froynt/mie • nuhr froyn • dihn*
my friend	**meinem Freund**
	mie • nuhm froynt
my friends	**meinen Freunden**
	mie • nuhn froyn • duhn
my colleague	**meinem Kollegen**
	mie • nuhm koh • leh • guhn
my colleagues	**meinen Kollegen**
	mie • nuhn koh • leh • guhn
When's your birthday?	**Wann haben Sie Geburtstag?**
	vahn hah • buhn zee guh • boorts • tahk
Are you married?	**Sind Sie verheiratet?**
	zihnt zee fehr • hie • rah • tuht
I'm…	**Ich bin …**
	eekh bihn …
single/in a relationship	**ledig/in einer Beziehung**
	leh • deek/ihn ien • uhr beh • tsee • oong
engaged	**verlobt**
	fehr • lohbt
married	**verheiratet**
	fehr • hie • rah • tuht
divorced	**geschieden**
	geh • shee • dehn
separated	**getrennt lebend**
	geh • trehnt leh • buhnd
widowed	**verwitwet**
	fehr • viht • veht

Do you have children/ grandchildren?	**Haben Sie Kinder/Enkelkinder?** *hah • buhn zee kihn • dehr/ ehn • kehl • kihn • dehr*

For Numbers, see page 22.

WORK & SCHOOL

What are you studying?	**Was studieren Sie?** *vahs shtoo • dee • ruhn zee*
I'm studying German.	**Ich studiere Deutsch.** *eekh shtoo • dee • ruh doych*
What do you do for a living?	**Was machen Sie beruflich?** *vahs mah • khuhn zee beh • roof • leekh*
I…	**Ich …** *eekh …*
work full-time/ part-time	**arbeite Vollzeit/Teilzeit** *ahr • bie • tuh fohl • tsiet/tiel • tsiet*
do freelance work	**bin Freiberufler** *bihn frie • beh • roo • flehr*
am a consultant	**bin Berater** *bihn beh • rah • tehr*
am unemployed	**bin arbeitslos** *bihn ahr • biets • lohs*
work at home	**arbeite zu Hause** *ahr • bie • tuh tsoo how • zuh*
Who do you work for?	**Für wen arbeiten Sie?** *fewr vehn ahr • bie • tuhn zee*
I work for…	**Ich arbeite für …** *eekh ahr • bie • tuh fewr …*
Here's my business card.	**Hier ist meine Visitenkarte.** *heer ihst mie • nuh vih • zee • tuhn • kahr • tuh*

For Communications, see page 86.

WEATHER

What's the forecast?	**Wie ist die Wettervorhersage?**
	vee ihst dee
	veh • tehr • fohr • hehr • zahg • uh
What beautiful/ terrible weather!	**Was für ein schönes/schlechtes Wetter!**
	vahs fewr ien sher • nuhs/shlehkht • uhs
	veh • tehr
It's…	**Es ist …**
	ehs ihst …
cool/warm	**kühl/warm**
	kewl/vahrm
cold/hot	**kalt/heiß**
	kahlt/hies
rainy/sunny	**regnerisch/sonnig**
	rehg • nuh • reesh/zoh • neek
There is snow/ice.	**Es gibt Schnee/Eis.**
	ehs gihbt shneh/ies
Do I need a jacket/ an umbrella?	**Brauche ich eine Jacke/einen Regenschirm?**
	brow • khuh eekh ien • uh yah • kuh/
	ien • uhn reh • guhn • sheerm

For Days, see page 26.

ON THE WAY

GETTING AROUND

NEED TO KNOW

How do I get to town?	**Wie komme ich in die Stadt?**
	vee koh • muh eekh ihn dee shtaht
Where's…?	**Wo ist …?**
	voh ihst …
the airport	**der Flughafen**
	dehr <u>flook</u> • hah • fuhn
the train [railway] station	**der Bahnhof**
	dehr <u>bahn</u> • hohf
the bus station	**die Bushaltestelle**
	dee <u>boos</u> • hahl • tuh • shteh • luh
the subway [underground] station	**die U-Bahn-Haltestelle**
	dee <u>oo</u> • bahn • <u>hahl</u> • tuh • shteh • luh
Is it far from here?	**Wie weit ist es?**
	vee viet ihst ehs
Where do I buy a ticket?	**Wo kann ich eine Fahrkarte kaufen?**
	voh kahn eekh <u>ie</u> • nuh <u>fahr</u> • kahr • tuh <u>kow</u> • fuhn

A one-way/ return ticket to…	**Ein Einzelticket/Eine Fahrkarte für Hin und Rückfahrt nach …**
	ien ien • tsehl • tee • kuht/ie • nuh fahr • kahr • tuh fewr hihn oond rewk • fahrt nahkh…
How much?	**Wie viel kostet es?**
	vee feel kohs • tuht ehs
Which gate/line?	**Welches Gate/Linie?**
	vehl • khehs geht/leen • yah
Which platform?	**Welcher Bahnsteig?**
	vehl • khehr bahn • shtieg
Where can I get a taxi?	**Wo finde ich ein Taxi?**
	voh fihn • duh eekh ien tahk • see
Take me to this address, please.	**Bitte fahren Sie mich zu dieser Adresse.**
	biht • tuh fah • ruhn zee meekh tsoo dee • zehr ah • dreh • suh
Can I have a map, please?	**Können Sie mir bitte einen Stadtplan geben?**
	ker • nuhn zee mihr biht • tuh ien • uhn shtaht • plahn geh • behn

TICKETS

When's…to Berlin?	**Wann geht … nach Berlin?**
	vahn geht … nahkh behr • leen
the (first) bus	**der (erste) Bus**
	dehr (ehr • stuh) boos
the (next) flight	**der (nächste) Flug**
	dehr (nehks • tuh) floog
the (last) train	**der (letzte) Zug**
	dehr (lehts • tuh) tsoog

Where do I buy...?	**Wo kaufe ich ...?**
	voh <u>kow</u> • fuh eekh ...
One/two airline ticket(s), please.	**Ein/Zwei Ticket(s), bitte.**
	ien/tsvie tee • kuht(s) <u>biht</u> • tuh
One/two (bus/train/ subway) ticket(s), please.	**Ein/Zwei Fahrkarte(n), bitte.**
	ien/tsvie <u>fahr</u> • kahr • tuh(n) <u>biht</u> • tuh
For today/tomorrow.	**Für heute/morgen.**
	fewr <u>hoy</u> • tuh/<u>mohr</u> • guhn
A...(airline) ticket.	**Ein ... Ticket.**
	ien ... <u>tee</u> • kuht
one-way	**einfaches**
	<u>ien</u> • fah • khuhs
return trip	**Hin- und Rückflug-**
	hihn oont <u>rewk</u> • floog
first class	**Erste-Klasse-**
	ehr • stuh • <u>klah</u> • suh
business class	**Business-Class-**
	<u>bihz</u> • nehs • klahs
economy class	**Economy-Class-**
	eh • <u>koh</u> • noh • mee • klahs
A...(bus/train/ subway) ticket.	**Eine ...**
	<u>ie</u> • nuh ...
one-way	**Einzelfahrkarte**
	<u>ien</u> • zuhl • fahr • karh • tuh
return trip	**Hin- und Rückfahrkarte**
	hihn oont <u>rewk</u> • fahr • kahr • tuh
first class	**Erste-Klasse-Fahrkarte**
	ehr • stuh • <u>klah</u> • suh • fahr • karh • tuh
How much?	**Wie viel kostet es?**
	vee feel <u>kohs</u> • tuht ehs
Can I buy a ticket on the bus/train?	**Kann ich im Bus/Zug eine Fahrkarte kaufen?**
	kahn eekh ihm boos/tsoog <u>ie</u> • nuh <u>fahr</u> • kahr • tuh <u>kow</u> • fuhn

I have an airline/ a train e-ticket.	**Ich habe ein E-Ticket/Online-Ticket.** *eekh hah • buh ien ay • tee • keht/* *ohn • lien • tee • keht*
Is there a discount for…?	**Gibt es eine Ermäßigung für …?** *gihpt ehs ie • nuh ehr • meh • see • goong* *fewr …*
children	**Kinder** *kihn • dehr*
students	**Studenten** *shtoo • dehn • tuhn*
senior citizens	**Rentner** *rehnt • nehr*
tourists	**Touristen** *too • rih • stuhn*
The express/local bus/train, please.	**Den Express-/Nahverkehrs-Bus/Zug,** **bitte.** *dehn ehks • prehs • /* *nah • fuhr • kehrs • boos/tsoog biht • tuh*
Do I have to stamp the ticket before boarding?	**Muss ich das Ticket vor dem** **Einsteigen entwerten?** *moos eekh dahs tihk • khet fohr dehm* *ayn • shtayg • uhn ehnt • vehr • thun*
How long is this ticket valid?	**Wie lange ist das Ticket gültig?** *vee lahng • uh ihst dahs tihk • khet* *gewl • teekh*
Can I return on the same ticket?	**Kann ich mit demselben Ticket** **zurückfahren?** *kahn eekh miht dehm • sehl • bhun* *tihk • khet tsoo • rewkh • fah • ruhn*
I'd like to… my reservation.	**Ich möchte meine Reservierung …** *eekh merkh • tuh mie • nuh* *reh • zehr • vee • roong …*
cancel	**stornieren** *shtohr • nee • ruhn*

change	**ändern**
	ehn • dehrn
confirm	**bestätigen**
	beh • shtay • tee • guhn

For Days, see page 26.

AIRPORT TRANSFER

How much is a taxi to the airport?	**Was kostet ein Taxi zum Flughafen?**
	vahs kohs • tuht ien tahk • see tsoom flook • hah • fuhn
To...Airport, please.	**Zum Flughafen ..., bitte.**
	tsoom flook • hah • fuhn ... biht • tuh
My airline is...	**Meine Fluggesellschaft ist ...**
	mie • nuh floo • geh • zehl • shahft ihst ...
My flight leaves at...	**Mein Flug geht um ...**
	mien floog geht oom ...
I'm in a rush.	**Ich habe es eilig.**
	eekh hah • buh ehs ie • leek
Can you take an alternate route?	**Können Sie eine andere Strecke fahren?**
	ker • nuhn zee ie • nuh ahn • deh • ruh shtreh • kuh fah • ruhn
Can you drive faster/slower?	**Können Sie schneller/langsamer fahren?**
	ker • nuhn zee shneh • lehr/ lahng • sah • mehr fah • ruhn

For Time, see page 25.

YOU MAY HEAR...

Mit welcher Fluggesellschaft fliegen Sie?
meet <u>vehlkh</u> • ehr <u>floog</u> • geh • sehl • shahft flee • gehn zee

Which airline are you flying?

Inland oder international?
<u>ihn</u> • lahnt <u>oh</u> • dehr ihn • tuhr • nah • syoh • <u>nahl</u>

Domestic or international?

Welcher Terminal?
<u>vehlkh</u> • ehr tehr • mee • <u>nahl</u>

What terminal?

YOU MAY SEE...

ANKUNFT	arrivals
ABFLUG	departures
GEPÄCKAUSGABE	baggage claim
INLANDSFLÜGE	domestic flights
INTERNATIONALE FLÜGE	international flights
CHECK-IN	check-in
E-TICKET CHECK-IN	e-ticket check-in
ABFLUG-GATES	departure gates

CHECKING IN

Where's check-in?	**Wo ist das Check-in?** *voh ihst dahs <u>tshehk</u> • in*
My name is...	**Mein Name ist ...** *mien <u>nahm</u> • uh ihst ...*

I'm going to…	**Ich reise nach …**
	eekh riez • uh nahkh …
I have…	**Ich habe …**
	eekh hahb • uh …
one suitcase	**einen Koffer**
	ien • uhn kohf • fehr
two suitcases	**zwei Koffer**
	tsvie kohf • fehr
one piece of hand luggage	**ein Handgepäckstück**
	ien hahnd • guh • pehk • shtewk
How much luggage is allowed?	**Wie viel Gepäck ist erlaubt?**
	vee feel guh • pehk ihst ehr • lowbt
Is that pounds or kilos?	**Sind das Pfund oder Kilo?**
	zihnt dahs pfoont oh • duhr kee • loh
Which terminal?	**Welcher Terminal?**
	vehlkh • ehr tehr • mee • nahl
Which gate?	**Welches Gate?**
	vehlkh • uhs geht
I'd like a window/ an aisle seat.	**Ich möchte gern einen Fensterplatz/ Platz am Gang.**
	eekh merkht • uh gehrn ien • uhn fehnst • ehr • plahts/plahts ahm gahng
When do we leave/arrive?	**Wann ist der Abflug/die Ankunft?**
	vahn ihst dehr ahp • floog/dee ahn • kuhnft
Is the flight delayed?	**Hat der Flug Verspätung?**
	haht dehr floog fehr • shpeh • toong
How late?	**Wie viel?**
	vee feel

LUGGAGE

Where is/are…?	**Wo ist/sind …?**
	voh ihst/zihnt …

the luggage trolleys	**die Gepäckwagen**
	dee guh • pehk • vah • guhn
the luggage lockers	**die Gepäckschließfächer**
	dee guh • pehk • shlees • fehkh • ehr

YOU MAY HEAR...

Der Nächste, bitte!	Next, please!
dehr nehkhst • uh biht • tuh	
Ihren Reisepass/Ihr Ticket, bitte.	Your passport/ ticket, please.
eehr • uhn riez • uh • pahs/eehr tih • kuht biht • tuh	
Geben Sie Gepäck auf?	Are you checking in any luggage?
gehb • ehn zee guh • pehk owf	
Das ist zu groß für Handgepäck.	That's too large for a carry-on [piece of hand luggage].
dahs ihst tsoo grohs fuehr hahnd • guh • pehk	
Haben Sie diese Taschen selbst gepackt?	Did you pack these bags yourself?
hah • buhn zee dees • uh tahsh • uhn sehlbst guh • pahkt	
Hat Ihnen jemand etwas mitgegeben?	Did anyone give you anything to carry?
haht eehn • uhn yeh • mahnd eht • vahs miht • guh • geh • buhn	
Leeren Sie Ihre Taschen.	Empty your pockets.
lehr • uhn zee eehr • uh tahsh • uhn	
Ziehen Sie Ihre Schuhe aus.	Take off your shoes.
tsee • uhn zee eehr • uh shoo • uh ows	
Wir beginnen jetzt mit dem Einsteigen...	We are now boarding...
weer beh • gihn • nuhn yehtst miht dehm ayn • shtayg • uhn ...	

the baggage claim	**die Gepäckausgabe**
	dee guh • pehk • ows • gahb • uh
My luggage has been lost/stolen.	**Mein Gepäck ist weg/wurde gestohlen.**
	mien guh • pehk ihst vehk/voor • duh
	guh • shtohl • uhn
My suitcase is damaged.	**Mein Koffer wurde beschädigt.**
	mien kohf • fehr voord • uh
	buh • shehd • eekht

FINDING YOUR WAY

Where is/are...?	**Wo ist/sind ...?**
	voh ihst/zihnt ...
the currency exchange	**die Wechselstube**
	dee vehkh • zuhl • shtoo • buh
the car hire	**die Autovermietung**
	dee ow • toh • fehr • meet • oong
the exit	**der Ausgang**
	dehr ows • gahng
the taxis	**die Taxis**
	dee tahks • ees
Is there a...into town?	**Gibt es ... in die Stadt?**
	gihbt ehs ... ihn dee shtadt
bus	**einen Bus**
	ien • uhn boos
train	**einen Zug**
	ien • uhn tsoog
subway [underground]	**eine U-Bahn**
	ien • uh oo • bahn

For Asking Directions, see page 66.

TRAIN

Where's the train [railway] station?	**Wo ist der Bahnhof?**
	voh ihst dehr <u>bahn</u> • hohf
How far is it?	**Wie weit ist es?**
	vee viet ihst ehs
Where is/are…?	**Wo ist/sind …?**
	voh ihst/zihnt …
the ticket office	**der Fahrkartenschalter**
	dehr <u>fahr</u> • kahrt • uhn • shahl • tehr
the information desk	**die Information**
	dee ihn • fohrm • ah • <u>syohn</u>
the luggage lockers	**die Gepäckschließfächer**
	dee guh • <u>pehk</u> • shlees • fehkh • ehr
the platforms	**die Bahnsteige**
	dee <u>bahn</u> • shtieg • uh
Can I have a schedule [timetable]?	**Kann ich einen Fahrplan haben?**
	kahn eehk <u>ien</u> • uhn <u>fahr</u> • plahn <u>hah</u> • buhn
How long is the trip?	**Wie lange dauert die Fahrt?**
	vee <u>lahng</u> • uh <u>dow</u> • ehrt dee fahrt
Is it a direct train?	**Ist das eine direkte Zugverbindung?**
	ihst dahs <u>ien</u> • uh dee • <u>rehkt</u> tsoog • ver • <u>bind</u> • ungh

---

YOU MAY SEE...

BAHNSTEIGE	platforms
INFORMATION	information
RESERVIERUNGEN	reservations
WARTERAUM	waiting room
ANKUNFT	arrivals
ABFAHRT	departures

German trains are fast, comfortable and reliable.
Train travel in Germany is a highly recommended alternative
to driving. The **Deutsche Bahn AG** is the national railway of
Germany. It offers many domestic and international routes.
Tickets can be purchased at the station or through a travel
agent. Buy your tickets in advance to get the cheapest fare
and to guarantee seating. Many reduced-fare options are
available; visit the **Deutsche Bahn AG** website or speak to a
travel agent for more information.

Do I have to change trains?	**Muss ich umsteigen?**
	moos eekh <u>oom</u> • shtieg • uhn
Is the train on time?	**Ist der Zug pünktlich?**
	ihst dehr tsoog <u>pewnkt</u> • leekh

For Numbers, see page 22.

DEPARTURES

Which track [platform] to…?	**Von welchem Bahnsteig fährt der Zug nach …?**
	fohn vehlkh • ehm bahn • shtieg fehrt dehr tsoog nahkh …
Is this the track [platform]/train to…?	**Ist das der Bahnsteig/Zug nach …?**
	ihst dahs dehr bahn • shtieg/tsoog nahkh …
Where is platform…?	**Wo ist Bahnsteig …?**
	voh ihst bahn • shtieg …
Where do I change for…?	**Wo steige ich um nach …?**
	voh shtieg • uh eekh oom nahkh …

YOU MAY HEAR…

Bitte einsteigen!	All aboard!
biht • tuh ien • shtieg • uhn	
Die Fahrkarten, bitte.	Tickets, please.
dee fahr • kahr • tuhn biht • tuh	
Sie müssen in … umsteigen.	You have to
zee mews • uhn ihn … oom • shtieg • uhn	change at…
Nächster Halt … Hauptbahnhof.	Next stop…
nehkh • stehr hahlt … howpt • bahn • hohf	

ON BOARD

Can I sit here?	**Kann ich mich hier hinsetzen?**
	kahn eekh meekh heer hihn • seht • suhn
Can I open the window?	**Kann ich das Fenster öffnen?**
	kahn eekh dahs fehn • stehr erf • nuhn

Is this seat available?	**Ist der Platz frei?**
	ihst dehr plahts frie
That's my seat.	**Das ist mein Platz.**
	dahs ihst mien plahts
Here's my reservation.	**Hier ist meine Reservierung.**
	heer ihst mien • uh reh • sehr • veer • roong

BUS

Where's the bus station?	**Wo ist die Bushaltestelle?**
	voh ihst dee boos • hahlt • uh • shtehl • uh
How far is it?	**Wie weit ist es?**
	vee viet ihst ehs
How do I get to…?	**Wie komme ich nach …?**
	vee kohm • uh eekh nahk…
Is this the bus to…?	**Ist das der Bus nach …?**
	ihst dahs dehr boos nahkh…
Can you tell me when to get off?	**Können Sie mir sagen, wann ich aussteigen muss?**
	kerhn • uhn zee meer zahg • uhn vahn eekh ows • shtieg • uhn moos

---

Bus and tram stops are marked by a green **H** for **Haltestelle** (stop). Larger cities, such as Berlin, Munich and Hamburg, offer 24-hour service. Service is limited on holidays and weekends.
In large German cities, the same ticket or pass can be used for the bus, subway, tram and above-ground train systems. Purchase tickets from the machines at bus stops or subway/tram stations. Check with a local travel agency or tourist information office about special discount tickets and offers.

Do I have to change buses?	**Muss ich umsteigen?**
	moos eekh <u>oom</u> • shtieg • uhn
Stop here, please!	**Bitte halten Sie hier!**
	biht • tuh <u>hahlt</u> • uhn zee heer

For Tickets, see page 47.

YOU MAY SEE...

BUSHALTESTELLE	bus stop
STOPP-TASTE	request stop
EINGANG/AUSGANG	enter/exit
FAHRSCHEIN ENTWERTEN	validate your ticket

METRO

Where's the U-Bahn [underground] station?	**Wo ist die U-Bahn-Haltestelle?**
	voh ihst dee <u>oo</u> • bahn • <u>halt</u> • uh • shtehl • uh
A map, please.	**Eine Übersichtskarte, bitte.**
	ien • nuh <u>ew</u> • behr • zehkhts • <u>kahr</u> • tuh biht • tuh
Which line for...?	**Welche Linie fährt nach ...?**
	<u>vehlkh</u> • uh lihn • ee • uh fehrt nahkh ...
Which direction?	**Welche Richtung?**
	<u>vehlkh</u> • uh reekh • toong
Do I have to transfer [change]?	**Muss ich umsteigen?**
	moos eekh oom • <u>shtieg</u> • uhn
Is this the U-Bahn [train] to...?	**Ist das die U-Bahn nach ...?**
	ihst dahs dee <u>oo</u> • bahn nahkh ...

YOU MAY SEE...

FAHRTZIEL	destination
EINZELFAHRT	one-trip ticket
TAGESKARTE	day pass
GRUPPENKARTE	group pass
WOCHENKARTE	weekly pass

How many stops to...?	**Wie viele Haltestellen sind es bis ...?**
	vee <u>feel</u> • uh <u>halt</u> • uh • shtehl • uhn zaht ehs bihs ...
Where are we?	**Wo sind wir?**
	voh zihnt veer

For Tickets, see page 47.

BOAT & FERRY

When is the ferry to...?	**Wann geht die Fähre nach ...?**
	vahn geht dee <u>fehr</u> • uh nahkh ...
Can I take my car?	**Kann ich mein Auto mitnehmen?**
	kahn eekh mien <u>ow</u> • toh <u>miht</u> • nehm • uhn
What time is the next sailing?	**Wann fährt das nächste Schiff ab?**
	vahn fehrt dahs <u>nehkh</u> • ste shihf ahb
Can I book a seat/cabin?	**Kann ich einen Sitzplatz/eine Kabine reservieren?**
	kahn eekh <u>ien</u> • uhn <u>sihts</u> • plahts/<u>ien</u> • uh kah • <u>bee</u> • nuh reh • sehr • <u>veer</u> • uhn
How long is the crossing?	**Wie lange dauert die Überfahrt?**
	vee <u>lahng</u> • uh <u>dow</u> • ehrt dee <u>ew</u> • behr • fahrt

For Weather, see page 43.

YOU MAY SEE…

RETTUNGSBOOT	life boat
SCHWIMMWESTE	life jacket

Ferry service across the Baltic Sea is available between Germany and Denmark, Sweden, Finland and Norway, or across the North Sea to the U.K. Ferry service is also available across Lake Constance to Austria and Switzerland. Boat trips are a fun way to explore the many rivers and lakes throughout Germany. Ferry and boat trips can be arranged by contacting your travel agent or searching the internet.

TAXI

Where can I get a taxi?	**Wo finde ich ein Taxi?** *voh fihnd • uh eekh ien tahk • see*
Can you send a taxi?	**Können Sie ein Taxi schicken?** *kern • nuhn zee ein tahk • see shihk • uhn*
Do you have the number for a taxi?	**Haben Sie die Telefonnummer für ein Taxi?** *hah • buhn zee dee tehl • uh • fohn • noom • ehr fewr ien tahk • see*
I'd like a taxi now/ for tomorrow at…	**Ich brauche jetzt/für morgen um … ein Taxi.** *eekh browkh • uh yehtst/fewr mohrg • uhn oom … ien tahk • see*

Pick me up at…	**Holen Sie mich um … ab.**
	hohl • uhn zee meekh oom … ahp
I'm going…	**Ich möchte …**
	eekh merkh • tuh …
to this address	**zu dieser Adresse**
	tsoo deez • ehr ah • drehs • suh
to the airport	**zum Flughafen**
	tsoom floog • hah • fuhn
to the train station	**zum Bahnhof**
	tsoom bahn • hohf
I'm late.	**Ich bin spät dran.**
	eekh bihn shpayt drahn
Can you drive faster/slower?	**Können Sie schneller/langsamer fahren?**
	kern • nuhn zee shnehl • ehr/ lahng • sahm • ehr fahr • uhn
Stop here.	**Halten Sie hier an.**
	hahl • tuhn zee heer ahn
Wait here.	**Warten Sie hier.**
	vahrt • uhn zee heer
How much?	**Wie viel kostet es?**
	vee feel kohs • tuht ehs
You said it would cost…	**Sie sagten, es würde … kosten.**
	zee zahg • tuhn ehs vewrd • uh … kohs • tuhn

Keep the change.	**Stimmt so.**
	shtihmt zoh
The receipt, please.	**Die Quittung, bitte.**
	dee kviht • oong biht • tuh

YOU MAY HEAR...

Wohin?	Where to?
voh • hihn	
Wie ist die Adresse?	What's the
wee ihst dee ah • drehs • uh	address?
Es wird ein Nachtzuschlag/	There's a
Flughafenzuschlag berechnet.	nighttime/
ehs veerd ien nahkht • tsoo • shlahg/	airport
floog • hahf • uhn • tsoo • shlahg	surcharge.
buh • rehkh • nuht	

You can catch a taxi at taxi stands, by calling to arrange for pick up, or by flagging down a passing available taxi. Taxi stands can be found at train stations, airports, large hotels and other popular areas in the city, such as shopping areas, parks and tourist destinations. Taxi service numbers can be found in the phone book or by asking your hotel concierge. All taxis are metered and will charge a base rate plus a rate per kilometer traveled. To tip the driver, round the fare up to the next euro or two, depending on the service.

BICYCLE & MOTORBIKE

I'd like to hire...	**Ich möchte gern ... mieten.**
	eekh merkh • tuh gehrn ... meet • uhn
a bicycle	**ein Fahrrad**
	ien fahr • raht
a moped	**ein Moped**
	ien moh • pehd
a motorbike	**ein Motorrad**
	ien moh • tohr • raht
How much per day/week?	**Wie viel pro Tag/Woche?**
	vee feel proh tahk/vohkh • uh
Can I have a helmet/lock?	**Kann ich einen Helm/ein Schloss haben?**
	kahn eekh ien • uhn hehlm/ien shlohs hah • buhn

CAR HIRE

Where's the car hire?	**Wo ist die Autovermietung?**
	voh ihst dee ow • toh • fehr • miet • oong
I'd like...	**Ich möchte ...**
	eekh merkh • tuh ...
a cheap/small car	**ein billiges/kleines Auto**
	ien bihl • lee • guhs/klien • uhs ow • toh
an automatic/ a manual car	**ein Auto mit Automatikschaltung/ Gangschaltung**
	ien ow • toh miht ow • toh • mah • teek • shahl • toong/ gahng • shahl • toong
air conditioning	**ein Auto mit Klimaanlage**
	ien ow • toh miht klee • mah • ahn • lah • guh
a car seat	**einen Kindersitz**
	ien • uhn kihnd • ehr • zihts

YOU MAY HEAR...

Haben Sie einen internationalen Führerschein?
hah • buhn zee ien • uhn ihnt • ehr • nah • syoh • nahl • uhn fewhr • uhr • shien

Do you have an international driver's license?

Ihren Reisepass, bitte.
eehr • uhn riez • uh • pahs biht • tuh

Your passport, please.

Möchten Sie eine Versicherung?
merkht • uhn zee ien • uh fehr • seekh • ehr • roong

Do you want insurance?

Ich benötige eine Anzahlung. *eekh buh • nert • ee • guh ien • uh ahn • tsah • loong*

I'll need a deposit.

Bitte unterschreiben Sie hier.
biht • tuh oont • ehr • shrieb • uhn zee heer

Sign here, please.

How much...?	**Wie viel kostet es ...?** *vee feel kohs • tuht ehs ...*
per day/week	**pro Tag/Woche** *proh tahk/vohkh • uh*
per kilometer	**pro Kilometer** *proh kee • loh • meh • tehr*
for unlimited mileage	**mit unbegrenzter Kilometerzahl** *miht oon • buh • grehnts • tuhr kee • loh • meh • tehr • tsahl*
with insurance	**mit Versicherung** *miht fehr • zeekh • ehr • oong*
Are there any discounts?	**Gibt es irgendwelche Ermäßigungen?** *gihpt ehs eer • guhnd • vehlkh • uh ehr • meh • see • goong • uhn*

FUEL STATION

Where's the fuel station?	**Wo ist die Tankstelle?** *voh ihst dee <u>tahnk</u> • shtehl • luh*
Fill it up, please.	**Bitte volltanken.** *<u>biht</u> • tuh <u>fohl</u> • tahnk • uhn*
…euros, please.	**… Euro, bitte. …** *<u>oy</u> • roh <u>biht</u> • tuh*
I'll pay in cash/by credit card.	**Ich bezahle bar/mit Kreditkarte.** *eekh beht • <u>sahl</u> • uh bahr/miht kreh • <u>deet</u> • kahr • tuh*

YOU MAY SEE…

BENZIN	gas [petrol]
BLEIFREI	unleaded
NORMAL	regular
SUPER	super
DIESEL	diesel

ASKING DIRECTIONS

Is this the way to…?	**Ist das der Weg nach …?** *ihst dahs dehr vehg nahkh …*
How far is it to…?	**Wie weit ist es bis …?** *vee viet ihst ehs bihs …*
Where's…?	**Wo ist …?** *voh ihst …*
Street	**die … Straße** *dee … <u>shtrahs</u> • suh*
this address	**diese Adresse** *<u>deez</u> • uh ah • <u>drehs</u> • uh*

the highway [motorway]	**die Autobahn**
	dee • uh ow • toh • bahn
Can you show me on the map?	**Können Sie mir das auf der Karte zeigen?**
	kern • nuhn zee meer dahs owf dehr kahrt • uh tsieg • uhn

YOU MAY HEAR...

geradeaus	straight ahead
geh • rahd • uh • ows	
links	left
leenks	
rechts	right
rehkhts	
an der/um die Ecke	on/around the corner
ahn dehr/oom dee eh • kuh	
gegenüber	opposite
geh • guhn • ew • behr	
hinter	behind
hihnt • ehr	
neben	next to
nehb • uhn	
nach	after
nahkh	
nördlich/südlich	north/south
nerd • leekh/zewd • leekh	
östlich/westlich	east/west
erst • leekh/vehst • leekh	
an der Ampel	at the traffic light
ahn dehr ahmp • ehl	
an der Kreuzung	at the intersection
ahn dehr kroytz • oong	

YOU MAY SEE...

(50)	**HÖCHSTGESCHWINDIGKEIT**	maximum speed limit
	ÜBERHOLVERBOT	no passing
	VERBOT FÜR FAHRZEUGE ALLER ART	all vehicles prohibited
	EINBAHNSTRASSE	one-way street
	KEINE DURCHFAHRT	no entry
STOP	**STOPP**	stop
	VORFAHRT GEWÄHREN	yield

I'm lost.	**Ich habe mich verfahren.**
	eekh hahb • uh meekh fehr • fahr • uhn

PARKING

Can I park here?	**Kann ich hier parken?**
	kahn eekh heer pahrk • uhn
Where's ...?	**Wo ist ...?**
	voh ihst ...
the parking garage	**das Parkhaus**
	dahs pahrk • hows
the parking lot [car park]	**der Parkplatz**
	dehr pahrk • plahts

Parking on the street is common in Germany; look for the sign showing a white letter 'P' on a blue background. You may see additional parking instructions located under the sign. The parking sign with the meter symbol indicates that you can park there for the amount of time shown (in hours - for example, **2 Std.** means 2 hours). Ask your rental car company for a parking disc when you pick up your car. Once parked, turn the dial to indicate the time you parked and put the disc on your dashboard where it is visible.

If you see a **mit Parkschein** sign you must buy a parking ticket from a nearby machine and place it on your dashboard where it is visible.

Parking lots and garages are other parking options. Most lots and garages use a self-pay system. When entering, obtain the time-stamped ticket from the machine. Use the machine near the pedestrian entrance to pay for parking; insert your ticket into the machine, pay the amount it displays and then remove the validated ticket. Proceed to your car and insert that ticket into the machine at the exit.

the parking meter	**die Parkuhr**
	dee pahrk • oor
How much…?	**Wie viel kostet es …?**
	vee feel kohs • tuht ehs …
per hour	**pro Stunde**
	proh shtoond • uh
per day	**pro Tag**
	proh tahk
for overnight	**über Nacht**
	ew • behr nahkht

BREAKDOWN & REPAIR

Where's the garage?	**Wo ist die Autowerkstatt?** *voh ihst dee ow • toh • <u>vehrk</u> • shtaht*
My car broke down/ won't start.	**Mein Auto ist kaputt/springt nicht an.** *mien <u>ow</u> • toh ihst <u>kah</u> • poot/shprihngt neekht ahn*
Can you fix it (today)?	**Können Sie es (heute) reparieren?** *<u>kern</u> • nuhn zee ehs (<u>hoy</u> • tuh) reh • pah • <u>reer</u> • uhn*
When will it be ready?	**Wann wird es fertig sein?** *vahn wirt ehs <u>fehr</u> • teekh zien*
How much?	**Wie viel kostet es?** *vee feel <u>kohs</u> • tuht ehs*
I have a puncture/ flat tyre (tire).	**Ich habe eine Reifenpanne.** *eekh hah • buh ien • uh rie • fehn • pahn • nuh*

ACCIDENTS

There was an accident.	**Es hat einen Unfall gegeben.** *ehs haht <u>ien</u> • uhn <u>oon</u> • fahl guh • <u>geh</u> • buhn*
Call an ambulance/ the police.	**Rufen Sie einen Krankenwagen/die Polizei.** *<u>roof</u> • uhn zee<u>ien</u> • uhn <u>krahnk</u> • uhn • vahg • uhn/dee poh • lee • <u>tsie</u>*

PLACES TO STAY

NEED TO KNOW

Can you recommend a hotel?	**Können Sie ein Hotel empfehlen?** _ker • nuhn zee ien hoh • tehl ehm • pfeh • luhn_
I have a reservation.	**Ich habe eine Reservierung.** _eekh hahb • uh ien • uh rehz • ehr • veer • oong_
My name is…	**Mein Name ist …** _mien nahm • uh ihst …_
Do you have a room…?	**Haben Sie ein Zimmer …?** _hah • buhn zee ien tsihm • mehr …_
for one person/ two people	**für eine Person/zwei Personen** _fewr ien • uh pehr • sohn/tsvie pehr • sohn • uhn_
with a bathroom	**mit Bad** _miht bahd_
with air conditioning	**mit Klimaanlage** _miht kleem • uh • ahn • lahg • uh_
For…	**Für …** _fewr …_
tonight	**heute Nacht** _hoy • tuh nahkht_
two nights	**zwei Nächte** _tsvie nehkht • uh_
one week	**eine Woche** _ien • uh vohkh • uh_
How much?	**Wie viel kostet es?** _vee feel kohs • tuht ehs_

Is there anything cheaper?	**Gibt es etwas Billigeres?**
	gihpt ehs <u>eht</u> • vahs <u>bihl</u> • lee • geh • ruhs
When's check-out?	**Wann ist der Check-out?**
	vahn ihst dehr <u>tshehk</u> • owt
Can I leave this in the safe?	**Kann ich das im Safe lassen?**
	kahn eekh dahs ihm sehf <u>lahs</u> • suhn
Can I leave my bags?	**Kann ich meine Taschen hierlassen?**
	kahn eekh <u>mien</u> • uh <u>tahsh</u> • uhn <u>heer</u> • lahs • suhn
Can I have my bill/a receipt?	**Kann ich meine Rechnung/eine Quittung haben?**
	kahn eekh <u>mien</u> • uh <u>rehkh</u> • noong/ <u>ien</u> • uh <u>kveet</u> • oong <u>hah</u> • buhn
I'll pay in cash/by credit card.	**Ich bezahle bar/mit Kreditkarte.**
	eekh beht • <u>sahl</u> • uh bahr/miht kreh • <u>deet</u> • kahr • tuh

SOMEWHERE TO STAY

Can you recommend…?	**Können Sie … empfehlen?**
	<u>kern</u> • uhn zee … ehm • <u>pfeh</u> • luhn
a hotel	**ein Hotel**
	ien hoh • <u>tehl</u>
a hostel	**eine Jugendherberge**
	<u>ien</u> • uh <u>yoog</u> • uhnd • hehr • behr • guh

If you didn't reserve accommodation before your
trip, visit the local **Touristeninformationsbüro** (tourist
information office) for recommendations on places to stay.

a campsite	**einen Campingplatz**
	ien • uhn kahmp • eeng • plahts
a bed and	**eine Pension**
breakfast	_ien • uh pehn • syohn_
What is near it?	**Was ist in der Nähe davon?**
	vahs ihst ihn dehr neh • uh dah • fohn
How do I get there?	**Wie komme ich dorthin?**
	vee kohm • uh eekh dohrt • hihn

AT THE HOTEL

I have a reservation.	**Ich habe eine Reservierung.**
	eekh hahb • uh ien • uh
	rehz • ehr • veer • oong
My name is…	**Mein Name ist …**
	mien nahm • uh ihst …
Do you have	**Haben Sie ein Zimmer …?**
a room…?	_hah • buhn zee ien tsihm • mehr …_
with a bathroom	**mit Bad/Dusche**
[toilet]/shower	_miht bahd/doo • shuh_
with air	**mit Klimaanlage**
conditioning	_miht kleem • uh • ahn • lah • guh_
that's smoking/	**für Raucher/Nichtraucher**
non-smoking	_fewr rowkh • ehr/neekht • rowkh • ehr_
For…	**Für …**
	fewr …
tonight	**heute Nacht**
	hoyt • uh nahkht
two nights	**zwei Nächte**
	tsvie nehkht • uh
a week	**eine Woche**
	ien • uh vohkh • uh
Do you have…?	**Haben Sie …?**
	hah • buhn zee …

YOU MAY HEAR...

Ihren Reisepass/Ihre Kreditkarte, bitte.	Your passport / credit card, please.
eehr • uhn _riez_ • uh • pahs/_eehr_ • uh	
kreh • _deet_ • kahrt • uh _biht_ • tuh	
Bitte füllen Sie dieses Formular aus.	Fill out this form, please.
biht • tuh _fewl_ • uhn zee _deez_ • uhs	
fohr • moo • _lahr_ ows	
Bitte unterschreiben Sie hier.	Sign here, please.
biht • tuh oon • tehr • _shrieb_ • uhn zee heer	

a computer	**einen Computer**
	ien • uhn kohm • _pjoot_ • ehr
an elevator [a lift]	**einen Fahrstuhl**
	ien • uhn _fahr_ • shtoohl
(wireless) internet service	**(wireless) Internetanschluss**
	(wier • luhs) _ihnt_ • ehr • neht • ahn • shloos
room service	**Zimmerservice**
	tsihm • mehr • sehr • vees
a pool	**einen Pool**
	ien • uhn pool
a gym	**einen Fitnessraum**
	ien • uhn _fiht_ • nehs • rowm
I need...	**Ich brauche ...**
	eekh _browkh_ • uh ...
an extra bed	**ein zusätzliches Bett**
	ien tsoo • _zehts_ • leeks • uhs beht
a cot	**ein Kinderbett**
	ien _kihnd_ • ehr • beht
a crib	**ein Gitterbett**
	ien _giht_ • tehr • beht

For Numbers, see page 22.

Travelers have numerous accommodation options in Germany, from budget to luxury. A **Pension** (bed and breakfast) provides opportunities to experience life in a German home. **Jugendherbergen** (youth hostels) are also available, catering to travelers of all ages. **Urlaub auf dem Bauernhof** (farm stay) is a great way to see the countryside and enjoy rural Germany. In some areas, you may be able to find **Modernisierte Schlossunterkünfte**, old castles that have been converted into beautiful accommodations. **Ferienwohnungen** (vacation apartments) and **Ferienhäuser** (holiday homes) allow travelers to rent fully equipped apartments and villas throughout Germany. All options can be booked with travel agents, tour companies or on the internet.

PRICE

How much per night/week?	**Wie viel kostet es pro Nacht/Woche?** *vee feel <u>kohs</u> • tuht ehs proh nahkht/ <u>vohk</u> • uh*
Does that include breakfast/sales tax [VAT]?	**Beinhaltet der Preis ein Frühstück/ Mehrwertsteuer?** *beh • <u>ien</u> • hahlt • uht dehr pries ien <u>frewh</u> • shtewkh/<u>mehr</u> • wehrt • shtoy • ehr*
Are there any discounts?	**Gibt es irgendwelche Ermäßigungen?** *gihpt ehs <u>eer</u> • guhnd • vehlkh • uh ehr • <u>meh</u> • see • goong • uhn*

PREFERENCES

Can I see the room?	**Kann ich das Zimmer sehen?** *kahn eekh dahs <u>tsihm</u> • mehr <u>zeh</u> • uhn*

I'd like a...room.	**Ich möchte ein ... Zimmer.**
	eekh merkh • tuh ien ... tsihm • muhr
better	**besseres**
	behs • sehr • uhs
bigger	**größeres**
	grers • ehr • uhs
cheaper	**billigeres**
	bihl • lee • gehr • uhs
quieter	**ruhigeres**
	roo • ee • gehr • uhs
I'll take it.	**Ich nehme es.**
	eekh nehm • uh ehs
No, I won't take it.	**Nein, ich nehme es nicht.**
	nien eekh nehm • uh ehs neekht

QUESTIONS

Where's...?	**Wo ist ...?**
	voh ihhst ...
the bar	**die Bar**
	dee bahr
the bathroom [toilet]	**die Toilette**
	dee toy • leht
the elevator [lift]	**der Fahrstuhl**
	dehr fahr • shtoohl
Can I have...?	**Kann ich ... haben?**
	kahn eekh ... hah • buhn
a blanket	**eine Decke**
	ien • uh dehk • uh
an iron	**ein Bügeleisen**
	ien bew • guh • liez • ehn
the room key/ the key card	**den Zimmerschlüssel/die Schlüsselkarte**
	dehn tsihm • mehr • shlews • uhl/dee shlews • ehl • kahrt • uh

YOU MAY SEE...

DRÜCKEN/ZIEHEN	push/pull
TOILETTE	bathroom [toilet]
DUSCHE	shower
FAHRSTUHL	elevator [lift]
TREPPE	stairs
WÄSCHEREI	laundry
BITTE NICHT STÖREN	do not disturb
FEUERSCHUTZTÜR	fire door
NOTAUSGANG	(emergency) exit
WECKRUF	wake-up call

a pillow	**ein Kissen**
	ien <u>kihs</u> • suhn
soap	**Seife**
	<u>zief</u> • uh
toilet paper	**Toilettenpapier**
	toy • <u>leht</u> • tuhn • pah • peer
a towel	**ein Handtuch**
	ien <u>hahnt</u> • tookh
Do you have an	**Haben Sie hierfür einen Adapter?**
	hah • buhn
adapter for this?	*zee heer • <u>fewr</u> ien • uhn ah • <u>dahp</u> • tehr*
How do I turn on	**Wie schalte ich das Licht an?**
the lights?	*vee <u>shahlt</u> • uh eekh dahs leekht ahn*
Can you wake	**Können Sie mich um ... wecken?**
	<u>kern</u> • nuhn
me at...?	*zee meekh oom ... <u>vehk</u> • uhn*
Can I leave this in	**Kann ich das im Safe lassen?**
the safe?	*kahn eekh dahs ihm sehf <u>lahs</u> • suhn*

Can I have my things from the safe?	**Kann ich meine Sachen aus dem Safe haben?**
	kahn eekh <u>mien</u> • uh <u>zahkh</u> • uhn ows dehm sehf <u>hah</u> • buhn
Is there mail [post]/ a message for me?	**Haben Sie Post/eine Nachricht für mich?**
	<u>hah</u> • buhn zee pohst/<u>ien</u> • uh <u>nahkh</u> • reekht fewr meekh
Do you have a laundry service?	**Bieten Sie einen Wäscheservice?**
	bih • tuhn zee ien • uhn vehsh • eh • ser • vice

PROBLEMS

There's a problem.	**Es gibt ein Problem.**
	ehs gihbt ien prohb • <u>lehm</u>
I lost my key/my key card.	**Ich habe meinen Schlüssel/meine Schlüsselkarte verloren.**
	eekh <u>hahb</u> • uh <u>mien</u> • uhn <u>shlews</u> • uhl/ <u>mien</u> • uh <u>shlews</u> • ehl • kahrt • uh fehr • <u>lohr</u> • uhn
I'm locked out of the room.	**Ich habe mich ausgesperrt.**
	eekh <u>hahb</u> • uh meekh ows • guh • <u>shpehrt</u>
There's no hot water/toilet paper.	**Ich habe kein heißes Wasser/ Toilettenpapier.**
	eekh <u>hahb</u> • uh kien <u>hies</u> • suhs <u>vahs</u> • sehr/<u>toy</u> • leht • uhn • pah • peer
The room is dirty.	**Das Zimmer ist schmutzig.**
	dahs <u>tsihm</u> • mehr ihst <u>shmoot</u> • seek
There are bugs in the room.	**Im Zimmer sind Insekten.**
	ihm <u>tsihm</u> • mehr zihnt ihn • <u>sehkt</u> • uhn

Voltage is 220, and plugs are two-pronged. You may need a converter and/or an adapter for your appliances.

The...doesn't work.	**... funktioniert nicht.**
	... foonk • syoh • <u>neert</u> neekht
Can you fix...?	**Können Sie ... reparieren?**
	<u>kern</u> • nuhn zee ... reh • pah • <u>reer</u> • ruhn
the air conditioning	**die Klimaanlage**
	dee <u>kleem</u> • uh • ahn • lahg • uh
the fan	**den Ventilator**
	dehn vehn • tee • <u>laht</u> • ohr
the heat [heating]	**die Heizung**
	dee <u>hiets</u> • oong
the light	**das Licht**
	dahs leekht
the TV	**den Fernseher**
	dehn <u>fehrn</u> • seh • ehr
the toilet	**die Toilette**
	dee toy • <u>leht</u> • tuh
I'd like another room.	**Ich möchte gern ein anderes Zimmer.**
	eekh <u>merkh</u> • tuh gehrn ien <u>ahn</u> • dehr • uhs <u>tsihm</u> • mehr

i

At hotels, it is common to leave tips for services provided. If you are happy with the housekeeping service, leave a tip of a few euros per day for the housekeeper in your room when you leave. The same applies for porters and your concierge generally too – a few euros when a service is provided is usual.

CHECKING OUT

Can I have an itemized bill/ a receipt?	**Kann ich eine aufgeschlüsselte Rechnung/Quittung haben?** *kahn eekh <u>ien</u>•uh owf•guh•<u>shlews</u>•ehlt•uh <u>rekh</u>•noong/ <u>kveet</u>•oong <u>hah</u>•buhn*
When's check-out?	**Wann ist der Check-out?** *vahn ihst dehr tshehk•owt*
Can I leave my bags here until…?	**Kann ich mein Gepäck bis … hierlassen?** *kahn eekh mien geh•<u>pehk</u> bihs … <u>heer</u>•lahs•uhn*
I think there's a mistake.	**Ich glaube, hier stimmt etwas nicht.** *eekh <u>glowb</u>•uh heer shtihmt <u>eht</u>•vahs neekht*
I'll pay in cash/by credit card.	**Ich bezahle bar/mit Kreditkarte.** *eekh beht•<u>sahl</u>•uh bahr/miht kreh•<u>deet</u>•kahrt•uh*

RENTING

I reserved an apartment/a room.	**Ich habe ein Apartment/ein Zimmer reserviert.** *eekh <u>hahb</u>•uh ien ah•<u>pahrt</u>•muhnt/ ien <u>tsihm</u>•mehr reh•sehr•<u>veert</u>*
My name is…	**Mein Name ist …** *mien <u>nahm</u>•uh ihst …*
Can I have the keys?	**Kann ich den Schlüssel haben?** *kahn eekh dehn <u>shlews</u>•suhl <u>hah</u>•buhn*
Are there…?	**Gibt es …?** *gihpt ehs …*
dishes	**Geschirr** *guh•<u>sheer</u>*

pillows	**Kissen**
	kihs • suhn
sheets	**Bettwäsche**
	beht • vehsh • uh
towels	**Handtücher**
	hahnt • tewkh • ehr
kitchen utensils	**Haushaltsgeräte**
	hows • hahlts • guh • reht • uh
When do I put out the bins/recycling?	**Wann stelle ich den Abfall/Müll raus?**
	vahn _shtehl_ • luh eekh dehn ahp • _fahl_/ mewl rows
…is broken.	**… funktioniert nicht.**
	… foonk • syoh • _neert_ neekht
How does…work?	**Wie funktioniert …?**
	vee foonk • syoh • _neert_ …
the air conditioner	**die Klimaanlage**
	dee _kleem_ • uh • ahn • lahg • uh
the dishwasher	**die Spülmaschine**
	dee _shpewl_ • mah • sheen • uh
the freezer	**der Gefrierschrank**
	dehr guh • _freer_ • shrahnk
the heating	**die Heizung**
	dee _hiet_ • soong
the microwave	**die Mikrowelle**
	dee mee • kroh • _vehl_ • luh
the refrigerator	**der Kühlschrank**
	dehr _kewhl_ • shrahnk
the stove	**der Herd**
	dehr hehrd
the washing machine	**die Waschmaschine**
	dee _vahsh_ • mah • shee • nuh

DOMESTIC ITEMS

I need...	**Ich brauche ...**
	eekh browkh • uh ...
an adapter	**einen Adapter**
	ien • uhn ah • dahp • tehr
aluminum [kitchen] foil	**Alufolie**
	ah • loo • foh • lee • uh
a bottle opener	**einen Flaschenöffner**
	ien • uhn flahsh • uhn • erf • nehr
a broom	**einen Besen**
	ien • uhn behz • uhn
a can opener	**einen Dosenöffner**
	ien • uhn doh • suhn • erf • nehr
cleaning supplies	**Reinigungsmittel**
	rien • ee • goongs • miht • tuhl
a corkscrew	**einen Korkenzieher**
	ien • uhn kohrk • uhn • tsee • ehr
detergent	**Waschmittel**
	vahsh • miht • tuhl
dishwashing liquid	**Geschirrspülmittel**
	guh • sheer • shpewl • miht • tuhl
bin bags	**Abfallsäcke**
	ahb • fahl • seh • khuh
a lightbulb	**eine Glühbirne**
	ien • uh glewh • beer • nuh
matches	**Streichhölzer**
	shtriekh • herlt • sehr
a mop	**einen Wischmopp**
	ien • uhn vihsh • mohp
napkins	**Servietten**
	sehr • vyeht • tuhn
paper towels	**Küchenrollen**
	kewkh • uhn • rohl • luhn

plastic wrap [cling film]	**Frischhaltefolie** *frihsh • hahl • tuh • foh • lee • uh*
a plunger	**eine Saugglocke** *ien • uh <u>zowg</u> • lohk • uh*
scissors	**eine Schere** *ien • uh <u>shehr</u> • uh*
a vacuum cleaner	**einen Staubsauger** *ien • uhn <u>shtowb</u> • sowg • ehr*

For In the Kitchen, see page 190.

AT THE HOSTEL

Is there a bed available?	**Haben Sie ein Bett frei?** *<u>hah</u> • buhn zee ien beht frie*
Can I have…?	**Kann ich … haben?** *kahn eekh … <u>hah</u> • buhn*
a single/double room	**ein Einzelzimmer/Doppelzimmer** *ien <u>ient</u> • sehl • tsihm • mehr/ <u>dohp</u> • pehl • tsihm • muhr*
a blanket	**eine Decke** *ien • uh <u>dehk</u> • huh*
a pillow	**ein Kissen** *ien <u>kihs</u> • suhn*
sheets	**Bettwäsche** *<u>beht</u> • vehsh • uh*
a towel	**ein Handtuch** *ien <u>hahnt</u> • tookh*
Do you have lockers?	**Haben Sie Schließfächer?** *<u>hah</u> • buhn zee <u>shlees</u> • fehkh • ehr*
When do you lock up?	**Wann schließen Sie ab?** *vahn <u>shlees</u> • suhn zee ahp*

ℹ️

There are more than 500 hostels throughout
Germany, in cities large and small and in rural locations. You
may need a Hostelling International membership card to
stay at these hostels, many of which belong to **Deutsches
Jugendherbergswerk (DJV)**. Hostels are inexpensive
accommodations that offer dormitory-style rooms and,
sometimes, private or semi-private rooms. Some offer
private bathrooms, though most have shared facilities.
There is usually a self-service kitchen on site. Booking in
advance is a good idea, especially in large cities during
festivals or holidays. Reservations can be made over the
phone or online. Visit the Hostelling International website
for more information.

Do I need a membership card?	**Brauche ich eine Mitgliedskarte?** _browkh • uh eekh ien • uh miht • gleeds • kahrt • uh_
Here's my international student card.	**Hier ist mein internationaler Studentenausweis.** _heer ihst mien ihn • tehr • nah • syoh • nahl • ehr shtoo • dehnt • uhn • ows • vies_

GOING CAMPING

Can I camp here?	**Kann ich hier campen?** _kahn eekh heer kahmp • uhn_
Where's the campsite?	**Wo ist der Campingplatz?** _voh ihst dehr kahmp • eeng • plahts_
What is the charge per day/week?	**Was kostet es pro Tag/Woche?** _vahs kohst • uht ehs proh tahk/vohkh • uh_
Are there…?	**Gibt es …?** _gihpt ehs …_

cooking facilities	**Kochmöglichkeiten**
	kohkh • merg • leekh • kiet • uhn
electric outlets	**Steckdosen**
	shtehkh • dohz • uhn
laundry facilities	**Waschmaschine**
	vahsh • maksch • een • uh
showers	**Duschen**
	doosh • uhn
tents for hire	**Mietzelte**
	meet • tsehl • tuh
Where can I empty the chemical toilet?	**Wo kann ich die Campingtoilette leeren?**
	voh kahn eekh dee
	kahmp • eeng • toy • leh • tuh lehr • uhn_

For Domestic Items, see page 82.

YOU MAY SEE...

TRINKWASSER	drinking water
ZELTEN VERBOTEN	no camping
OFFENES FEUER VERBOTEN	no fires

COMMUNICATIONS

NEED TO KNOW

Where's an internet cafe?	**Wo gibt es ein Internetcafé?** *voh gihpt ehs ien* *ihnt • ehr • neht • kah • feh*
Can I access the internet/check e-mail?	**Kann ich das Internet benutzen/ meine E-Mails lesen?** *kahn eekh dahs ihnt • ehr • neht* *beh • noot • suhn/mien • uh ee • miels* *lehz • uhn*
How much per (half) hour?	**Wie viel kostet eine (halbe) Stunde?** *vee feel kohst • uht ien • uh (hahlb • uh)* *shtoond • uh*
How do I log on?	**Wie melde ich mich an?** *vee mehld • uh eekh meekh ahn*
A phone card, please.	**Eine Telefonkarte, bitte.** *ien • uh tehl • uh • fohn • kahrt • uh* *biht • tuh*
Can I have your phone number?	**Kann ich Ihre Telefonnummer haben?** *kahn eekh eehr • uh* *tehl • uh • fohn • noom • ehr hah • buhn*
Here's my number/e-mail.	**Hier ist meine Telefonnummer/ E-Mail.** *heer ihst mien • uh* *tehl • uh • fohn • noom • ehr/ ee • miel*
Call me.	**Rufen Sie mich an.** *roo • fuhn zee meekh ahn*
E-mail me.	**Mailen Sie mir.** *miel • uhn zee meer*

Hello. This is…	**Hallo. Hier ist …**
	hah • loh heer ihst …
Can I speak to…?	**Kann ich mit … sprechen?**
	kahn eekh miht … shprehkh • uhn
Can you repeat that, please?	**Könnten Sie das bitte wiederholen?**
	kern • tuhn zee dahs biht • tuh veed • ehr • hohl • uhn
I'll call back later.	**Ich rufe später zurück.**
	eekh roof • uh shpeht • ehr tsoo • rewkh
Bye.	**Auf Wiederhören.**
	owf veed • ehr • her • ruhn
Where's the post office?	**Wo ist die Post?**
	voh ihst dee pohst
I'd like to send this to…	**Ich möchte das nach … schicken.**
	eekh merkh • tuh dahs nahkh … shihk • uhn

ONLINE

Where's an internet cafe?	**Wo gibt es ein Internetcafé?**
	voh gihpt ehs ien ihnt • ehr • neht • kah • feh
Does it have wireless internet?	**Gibt es dort wireless Internet?**
	gihpt ehs dohrt wier • luhs ihnt • ehr • neht
What is the WiFi password?	**Wie lautet das WLAN-Passwort?**
	vee low • teht dahs veh • lahn • pahs • vohrt
Is the WiFi free?	**Ist der WLAN-Zugang gratis?**
	ihst dehr veh • lahn • tsoo • gahng grah • tihs
Do you have bluetooth?	**Haben Sie Bluetooth?**
	hah • buhn zee bloo • tooth
How do I turn the computer on/off?	**Wie schalte ich den Computer an/aus?**
	vee shahlt • uh eekh dehn kohm • pjoot • ehr ahn/ows

Can I...?	**Kann ich ...?**
	kahn eekh ...
access the internet	**das Internet benutzen**
	dahs ihnt•ehr•neht beh•noot•suhn
check e-mail	**E-Mails lesen**
	ee•miels lehz•uhn
print	**drucken**
	drook•uhn
plug in/charge my laptop/iPhone/ iPad/BlackBerry?	**meinen Laptop/mein iPhone/iPad/ BlackBerry aufladen?**
	kahn eehk mien•uhn lap•top/mien iphone/ipad/blackberry owf•lahd•uhn
access Skype?	**Skype verwenden?**
	skype fuhr•vehn•dehn
use any computer	**einen Computer benutzen**
	ien•uhn kohm•pjoot•ehr beh•noot•suhn
How much per (half) hour?	**Wie viel kostet eine (halbe) Stunde?**
	vee feel kohst•uht ien•uh (hahlb•uh) shtoond•uh
How...?	**Wie ...?**
	vee ...
do I connect	**stelle ich eine Verbindung her**
	shteh•luh eekh ien•uh fuhr•bihnd•oong hehr
do I disconnect	**trenne ich eine Verbindung**
	trehn•uh eekh ien•uh fuhr•bihnd•oong
do I log on/off	**melde ich mich an/ab**
	mehld•uh eekh meekh ahn/ahp
do I type this symbol	**gebe ich dieses Zeichen ein**
	geh•buh eekh deez•uhs tsiekh•ehn ien
What's your e-mail?	**Wie ist Ihre E-Mail-Adresse?**
	vee ihst eehr•uh ee•miel•ah•drehs•uh
My e-mail is...	**Meine E-Mail-Adresse ist ...**
	mien•uh ee•miel•ah•drehs•uh ihst ...

Do you have a scanner?

Haben Sie einen Scanner?
hah • buhn zee ien • uhn scan • nuhr

YOU MAY SEE...

SCHLIESSEN	close
LÖSCHEN	delete
E-MAIL	e-mail
BEENDEN	exit
HILFE	help
INSTANT MESSENGER	instant messenger
INTERNET	internet
ANMELDEN	login
NEUE NACHRICHT	new message
AN/AUS	on/off
ÖFFNEN	open
DRUCKEN	print
SPEICHERN	save
SENDEN	send
BENUTZERNAME/PASSWORT	username/ password
WIRELESS INTERNET	wireless internet

SOCIAL MEDIA

Are you on Facebook/Twitter?	**Sind Sie bei Facebook/Twitter?** (polite form) *zihnt zee by face • book/twit • ter* **Bist du bei Facebook/Twitter?** (informal form) *bihst doo by face • book/twit ter*
What's your user name?	**Was ist Ihr Benutzername?** (polite form) *vahs ihst eehr beh • noots • uhr • nah • muh* **Was ist dein Benutzername?** (informal form) *vahs ihst dien beh • noots • uhr • nah • muh*
I'll follow you on Twitter.	**Ich werde Ihre Twitter-Einträge verfolgen.** (polite form) *eekh vehr • duh eer • he twit • ter • ien • treh • ghe fehr • folg • hun* **Ich werde deine Twitter-Einträge verfolgen.** (informal form) *eekh vehr • duh die • nuh twit • ter • ien • treh • ghe fehr • folg • hun*
Are you following...?	**Verfolgen Sie ...?** (polite form) *fehr • folg • hun zee ...* **Verfolgst du ...?** (informal form) *fehr • folgst doo ...*
I'll add you as a friend.	**Ich werde Sie als Freund/Freundin hinzufügen.** (polite form) *eekh vehrd • uh zee ahls froynd/ froyn • dihn hihn • tsoo • few • guhn* **Ich werde dich als Freund/Freundin hinzufügen.** (informal form) *eekh vehrd • uh deekh ahls froynd/ froyn • dihn hihn • tsoo • few • guhn*

I'll put the pictures on Facebook/Twitter.	**Ich werde die Fotos auf Facebook/ Twitter hochladen.**
	eekh vehr • duh dee foh • tohs owf face • book/ twit • ter hokh • lah • duhn
I'll tag you in the pictures.	**Ich werde Sie auf den Fotos markieren.** *(polite form)*
	eekh vehr • duh zee owf dehn foh • tohs mahr • kih • ruhn
	Ich werde dich auf den Fotos markieren. *(informal form)*
	eekh vehr • duh deekh owf dehn foh • tohs mahr • kih • ruhn

YOU MAY SEE...

SCHLIESSEN	close
LÖSCHEN	delete
E-MAIL	e-mail
BEENDEN	exit
HILFE	help
INSTANT MESSENGER	instant messenger
INTERNET	internet
ANMELDEN	login
NEUE NACHRICHT	new message
AN/AUS	on/off
ÖFFNEN	open
DRUCKEN	print
SPEICHERN	save
SENDEN	send
BENUTZERNAME/PASSWORT	username/ password
WIRELESS INTERNET	wireless internet

PHONE

A phone card, please.	**Eine Telefonkarte, bitte.** _ien • uh tehl • eh • <u>fohn</u> • kahrt • uh <u>biht</u> • tuh_
A prepaid phone please.	**Ein Prepaid-Handy, bitte.** _ien pree • paid han • dee biht • tuh_
An international phonecard for…	**Eine internationale Telefonkarte für …** _<u>ien</u> • uh ihnt • ehr • nah • syoh • <u>nahl</u> • uh tehl • uh • <u>fohn</u> • kahrt • uh fewr …_
Australia	**Australien** _ow • <u>shtrah</u> • lee • ehn_
Canada	**Kanada** _<u>kah</u> • nah • dah_
Ireland	**Irland** _eer • lahnt_
the U.K.	**Großbritannien** _grohs • bree • <u>tahn</u> • ee • ehn_
the U.S.	**die USA** _dee <u>oo</u> • ehs • ah_
How much?	**Wie viel kostet es?** _vee feel <u>kohs</u> • tuht ehs_
Where's the pay phone?	**Wo ist das Münztelefon?** _voh ihst dahs mewnts • tehl • uh • fohn_
What's the area code/country code for…?	**Was ist die Ortsvorwahl/Landesvorwahl für …?** _vahs ihst dee <u>ohrts</u> • fohr • vahl/ <u>lahnd</u> • uhs • fohr • vahl fewr …_
What's the number for Information?	**Was ist die Nummer für die Auskunft?** _vahs ihst dee <u>noom</u> • ehr fewr dee ows • kuhnft_
I'd like the number for…	**Ich hätte gern die Nummer für …** _eekh <u>heht</u> • uh gehrn dee <u>noom</u> • ehr fewr …_

I'd like to call collect [reverse the charges].
Ich möchte ein R-Gespräch führen.
eekh merkh • tuh ien ehr • guh • shprehkh fewhr • uhn

My phone doesn't work here.
Mein Telefon funktioniert hier nicht.
mien tehl • leh • fohn foonk • syoh • neert heer neekht

What network are you on?
Welches Netz nutzen Sie?
vehl • khehs nehts noot • suhn zee

YOU MAY HEAR...

Ruff an?
roof ahn
Who's calling?

Einen Moment, bitte.
ien • uhn moh • mehnt biht • tuh
Hold on, please.

Ich verbinde Sie.
eekh fehr • bihnd • uh zee
I'll put you through.

Er m /Sie f ist nicht da/spricht gerade.
ehr/zee ihst neekht dah/shpreekht geh • rahd • uh
He/She is not here/on another line.

Möchten Sie eine Nachricht hinterlassen?
merkh • tuhn zee ien • uh nahkh • reekht hihnt • ehr • lahs • suhn
Would you like to leave a message?

Bitte rufen Sie später/in zehn Minuten zurück.
biht • tuh roof • uhn zee shpeht • ehr/ihn tsehn mee • noot • uhn tsoo • rewkh
Please call back later/in ten minutes.

Kann er m /sie f zurückrufen?
khan ehr/zee tsoo • rewkh • roof • uhn
Can he/she call you back?

Was ist Ihre Nummer?
vahs ihst eehr • uh noom • ehr
What's your number?

Is it 3G?	**Ist es ein 3G-Netz?**
	ihst ehs ien drie • geh • nehts
I have run out of credit/minutes.	**Ich habe kein Guthaben mehr.**
	eekh hah • buh kien goot • hah • buhn mehr
Can I buy some credit?	**Kann ich eine Guthabenkarte kaufen?**
	kahn eekh ie • nuh
	goot • hah • buhn • kahr • tuh kow • fuhn
Do you have a phone charger?	**Haben Sie ein Handy-Ladegerät?**
	hah • buhn zee ien
	han • dee • lah • duh • guh • reht
Can I recharge this phone?	**Kann ich dieses Telefon wieder aufladen?**
	kahn eekh <u>deez</u> • uhs tehl • uh • <u>fohn</u> <u>veed</u> • ehr owf • <u>lahd</u> • uhn
Can I have your number, please?	**Können Sie mir bitte Ihre Nummer geben?**
	<u>kern</u> • uhn zee meer <u>biht</u> • tuh <u>eehr</u> • uh <u>noom</u> • ehr <u>gehb</u> • uhn

German public phones are mainly card operated. Phone cards in various amounts can be purchased at newsstands, supermarkets and other shops.
Important telephone numbers include:
Police 110
Fire 112
Ambulance 115
National Directory 11833
National Directory (in English) 11837
International Directory 11834
To call the U.S. or Canada from Germany, dial 001 + area code + phone number. To call the U.K. from Germany, dial 0044 + area code (minus the first 0) + phone number.

Here's my number.	**Hier ist meine Nummer.**
	heer ihst <u>mien</u> • uh <u>noom</u> • ehr
Please call me.	**Bitte rufen Sie mich an.**
	<u>biht</u> • tuh <u>roof</u> • uhn zee meekh ahn
Please text me.	**Bitte schicken Sie mir eine SMS.**
	bit • tuh <u>shihk</u> • uhn zee meer <u>ien</u> • uh
	ehs • ehm • ehs
I'll call you.	**Ich werde Sie anrufen.**
	eekh <u>vehrd</u> • uh zee <u>ahn</u> • roof • uhn
I'll text you.	**Ich werde Ihnen eine SMS schicken.**
	eekh <u>vehrd</u> • uh <u>eehn</u> • uhn <u>ien</u> • uh
	ehs • ehm • ehs <u>shihk</u> • uhn

TELEPHONE ETIQUETTE

Hello. This is…	**Hallo. Hier ist …**
	<u>hahl</u> • loh heer ihst …
Can I speak to…?	**Kann ich mit … sprechen?**
	kahn eekh miht … <u>shprehkh</u> • uhn
Extension…	**Durchwahl …**
	<u>doorkh</u> • vahl …
Speak louder/more slowly, please.	**Bitte sprechen Sie lauter/langsamer.**
	<u>biht</u> • tuh <u>shprehkh</u> • uhn zee <u>lowt</u> • ehr/ <u>lahng</u> • sahm • ehr
Can you repeat that, please?	**Könnten Sie das bitte wiederholen?**
	<u>kern</u> • tuhn zee dahs <u>biht</u> • tuh vee • dehr • <u>hohl</u> • uhn
I'll call back later.	**Ich rufe später zurück.**
	eekh <u>roof</u> • uh <u>shpeht</u> • ehr <u>tsoo</u> • rewkh
Bye.	**Auf Wiederhören.**
	owf <u>veed</u> • ehr • her • ruhn

For Communications, see page 86.

FAX

Can I send/receive a fax here?	**Kann ich hier ein Fax senden/ empfangen?**
	kahn eekh heer ien fahks <u>zehnd</u> • uhn/ ehm • pfahng • uhn
What's the fax number?	**Was ist die Faxnummer?**
	vahs ihst dee <u>fahks</u> • noom • ehr
Please fax this to…	**Bitte faxen Sie das nach …**
	<u>biht</u> • tuh <u>fahks</u> • uhn zee dahs nahkh …

POST

Where's the post office/mailbox?	**Wo ist die Post/der Briefkasten?**
	voh ihst dee pohst/dehr <u>breef</u> • kahs • tuhn
A stamp for this postcard/letter to…, please.	**Eine Briefmarke für diese Postkarte/ diesen Brief nach … bitte.**
	ien • uh <u>breef</u> • mahrk • uh fewr <u>deez</u> • uh pohst • kahrt • uh/<u>deez</u> • uhn breef nahkh … biht • tuh
How much?	**Wie viel kostet das?**
	vee feel <u>kohs</u> • tuht dahs

YOU MAY HEAR...

Bitte füllen Sie das Zollformular aus.
biht • _tuh fewl_ • _luhn zee dahs_
tsohl • _fohr_ • _moo_ • _lahr ows_

Fill out the customs declaration form, please.

Wie viel ist es wert?
vee feel ihst ehs vehrt

What's the value?

Was ist der Inhalt?
vahs ihst dehr ihn • _hahlt_

What's inside?

Please send this package by airmail/express.

Senden Sie dieses Paket bitte per Luftpost/Express.
zehnd • _uhn zee deez_ • _uhs pah_ • _keht_
biht • _tuh pehr looft_ • _pohst/ehks_ • _prehs_

A receipt, please.

Eine Quittung, bitte.
ien • _uh kveet_ • _toong biht_ • _tu_

In addition to mailing options, German post offices offer a variety of other services. Most provide banking services and allow you to deposit or withdraw money and apply for a credit card. On weekdays, post offices are usually open from 8:30 a.m. to 1:00 p.m., and again from 2:30 p.m. to 4:00 p.m. (in larger cities to 6:30 p.m.). On Saturdays they are open from 8:30 a.m. to 1:00 p.m.

SIGHTSEEING

NEED TO KNOW

Where's the tourist information office?	**Wo ist das Touristeninformationsbüro?** *voh ihst dahs* *too • <u>ree</u> • stuhn • een • fohr • mah • syohns • bew • roh*
What are the main sights?	**Was sind die wichtigsten Sehenswürdigkeiten?** *vahs zihnt dee <u>veekh</u> • teeg • stuhn <u>zeh</u> • uhns • vewr • deekh • kie • tuhn*
Do you offer tours in English?	**Haben Sie Führungen in Englisch?** *<u>hah</u> • buhn zee <u>few</u> • roong • uhn een ehn • gleesh*
Can I have a map/ guide?	**Kann ich einen Stadtplan/ Reiseführer haben?** *kahn eekh <u>ien</u> • uhn <u>shtaht</u> • plahn/ rie • seh • <u>fewhr</u> • ehr <u>hah</u> • buhn*

TOURIST INFORMATION

Do you have information on...?
Haben Sie Informationen über ...?
hah • buhn zee
ihn • fohr • mah • syoh • nuhn ew • buhr ...

Can you recommend...?
Können Sie ... empfehlen?
ker • nuhn zee ... ehm • pfeh • luhn

  a bus tour
eine Busreise
ien • uh boos • rie • zuh

  an excursion to...
einen Ausflug nach ...
ien • uhn ows • flook nahkh ...

  a sightseeing tour
eine Stadtrundfahrt
ien • uh shtaht • roond • fahrt

ON TOUR

I'd like to go on the tour to...
Ich möchte gern an der ... Führung teilnehmen.
eekh merkht • uh gehrn ahn dehr ...
fewhr • oong tiel • nehm • uhn

When's the next tour?
Wann ist die nächste Führung?
vahn ihst dee nehkhst • uh fewhr • oong

Are there tours in English?
Gibt es Führungen in Englisch?
gihpt ehs fewhr • oong • uhn ihn
ehng • lihsh

Is there an English guide book/audio guide?
Gibt es einen englischsprachigen Reiseführer/Audio-Guide?
gihpt ehs ien • uhn
ehng • lihsh • shprahkh • ee • guhn
riez • uh • fewhr • ehr/ow • dee • oh • gied

What time do we leave/return?
Wann fahren wir ab/kommen wir wieder?
vahn fahhr • uhn veer ap/kohm • uhn veer
veed • ehr

We'd like to see…	**Wir möchten gern … sehen.**
	veer merkht • uhn gehrn … zeh • uhn
Can we stop here…?	**Können wir hier anhalten …?**
	ker • nuhn veer heer ahn • hahlt • uhn …
to take photos	**um Fotos zu machen**
	oom foht • ohs tsoo mahkh • uhn
for souvenirs	**um Andenken zu kaufen**
	oom ahn • dehnk • uhn tsoo kowf • uhn
for the toilets	**um auf die Toilette zu gehen**
	oom owf dee toy • leht • uh tsoo geh • uhn
Is it disabled-accessible?	**Ist es behindertengerecht?**
	ihst ehs beh • hihn • dehrt • uhn • geh • rehkht

For Tickets, see page 47.

SEEING THE SIGHTS

Where's…?	**Wo ist …?**
	voh ihst …
the battleground	**das Schlachtfeld**
	dahs shlahkht • fehlt
the botanical garden	**der botanische Garten**
	dehr boh • tahn • eesh • uh gahr • tuhn
the castle	**das Schloss**
	dahs shlohs
the downtown area	**das Stadtzentrum**
	dahs shtadt • tsehnt • room
the fountain	**der Brunnen**
	dehr broon • uhn
the library	**die Bücherei**
	dee bewkh • eh • rie
the market	**der Markt**
	dehr mahrkt
the museum	**das Museum**
	dahs moo • zeh • oom

Tourist information offices are located throughout Germany. Look for the 'i' symbol or ask your hotel concierge where the nearest office is located. Tourist information offices can recommend destinations, attractions, local events and festivals, and help you find hotels, tours, transportation and other services. Visit the **Deutsche Zentrale für Tourismus**, **DZT** (German center for tourism), website for more information.

the old town	**die Altstadt**
	dee <u>ahlt</u> • shtahdt
the opera house	**das Opernhaus**
	dahs <u>oh</u> • pehrn • hows
the palace	**der Palast**
	dehr pah • <u>lahst</u>
the park	**der Park**
	dehr pahrk
the ruins	**die Ruine**
	dee ro • <u>ee</u> • nuh
the shopping area	**das Einkaufszentrum**
	dahs <u>ien</u> • kowfs • tsehn • troom
the theater	**das Theater**
	dahs teh • <u>ah</u> • tehr
the tower	**der Turm**
	dehr toorm
the town hall	**das Rathaus**
	dahs <u>raht</u> • hows
the town square	**der Rathausplatz**
	dehr <u>raht</u> • hows • plats

Can you show me on the map?	**Können Sie mir das im Stadtplan zeigen?**
	ker • _nuhn zee meer dahs ihm_
	shtadt • _plahn_ _tsie_ • _guhn_
It's...	**Es ist ...**
	ehs ihst ...
amazing	**erstaunlich**
	ehr • _shtown_ • _leekh_
beautiful	**wunderschön**
	voond • _ehr_ • _shern_
boring	**langweilig**
	lahng • _viel_ • _eek_
interesting	**interessant**
	ihn • _teh_ • _reh_ • _sahnt_
magnificent	**großartig**
	groh • _sahr_ • _teek_
romantic	**romantisch**
	roh • _mahnt_ • _eesh_
strange	**seltsam**
	zehlt • _zahm_
stunning	**umwerfend**
	oom • _vehrf_ • _uhnt_
terrible	**schrecklich**
	shrehk • _leekh_
ugly	**hässlich**
	hehs • _leekh_
I (don't) like it.	**Es gefällt mir (nicht).**
	ehs guh • _fehlt_ _meer (neekht)_

For Grammar, see page 12.

RELIGIOUS SITES

Where's...?	**Wo ist ...?**
	voh ihst ...
the cathedral	**die Kathedrale**
	dee kah • teh • <u>drahl</u> • uh
the Catholic/	**die katholische/evangelische Kirche**
Protestant church	*dee kah • <u>toh</u> • leesh • uh/*
	eh • vahn • <u>gehl</u> • eesh • uh keer • khuh
the mosque	**die Moschee**
	dee moh • <u>sheh</u>
the shrine	**der Schrein**
	dehr shrien
the synagogue	**die Synagoge**
	dee zewn • uh • <u>goh</u> • guh
the temple	**der Tempel**
	dehr <u>tehm</u> • pehl
What time is mass/	**Wann ist die Messe/der Gottesdienst?**
the service?	*vahn ihst dee <u>mehs</u> • suh/dehr*
	<u>goht</u> • ehs • deenst

LEISURE TIME

SHOPPING

NEED TO KNOW

Where's the market/ mall [shopping centre]?	**Wo ist der Markt/das Einkaufszentrum?** *voh ihst dehr mahrkt/dahs ien • kowfs • tsehn • troom*
I'm just looking.	**Ich schaue mich nur um.** *eekh show • uh meekh noor oom*
Can you help me?	**Können Sie mir helfen?** *kern • uhn zee meer hehlf • uhn*
I'm being helped.	**Ich werde schon bedient.** *eekh vehrd • uh shohn beh • deent*
How much?	**Wie viel kostet das?** *vee feel kohs • tuht dahs*
That one, please.	**Dieses bitte.** *dee • zuhs biht • tuh*
That's all.	**Das ist alles.** *dahs ihst ahl • uhs*
Where can I pay?	**Wo kann ich bezahlen?** *voh kahn eekh beh • tsahl • uhn*
I'll pay in cash/by credit card.	**Ich zahle bar/mit Kreditkarte.** *eekh tsahl • uh bahr/miht kreh • deet • kahr • tuh*
A receipt, please.	**Eine Quittung, bitte.** *ien • uh kvih • toong biht • tuh*

AT THE SHOPS

Where's…?	**Wo ist …?** *voh ihst …*

the antiques store	**das Antiquitätengeschäft** *dahs ahn • tee • kwee • tay • tuhn • guh • shehft*
the bakery	**die Bäckerei** *dee beh • keh • rie*
the bank	**die Bank** *dee bahnk*
the bookstore	**der Buchladen** *dehr bookh • lahd • uhn*
the clothing store	**das Bekleidungsgeschäft** *dahs buh • klied • oongs • guh • shehft*
the delicatessen	**das Feinkostgeschäft** *dahs fien • kohst • guh • shehft*
the department store	**das Kaufhaus** *dahs kowf • hows*
the gift shop	**der Geschenkwarenladen** *dehr guh • shehnk • vah • ruhn • lah • duhn*
the health food store	**das Reformhaus** *dahs reh • fohrm • hows*
the jeweler	**das Schmuckgeschäft** *dahs shmook • guh • shehft*
the liquor store [off-licence]	**das Spirituosengeschäft** *dahs shpee • ree • twoh • zuhn • guh • shehft*
the market	**der Markt** *dehr mahrkt*
the music store	**das Musikgeschäft** *dahs moo • zeek • guh • shehft*
the pastry shop	**die Konditorei** *dee kohn • dee • toh • rie*
the pharmacy [chemist]	**die Apotheke** *dee ah • poh • tehk • uh*
the produce [grocery] store	**das Lebensmittelgeschäft** *dahs lehb • uhns • miht • uhl • guh • shehft*
the shoe store	**das Schuhgeschäft** *dahs shooh • guh • shehft*

the shopping mall [shopping centre]	**das Einkaufszentrum**
	dahs ien • kowfs • tsehn • troom
the souvenir store	**der Andenkenladen**
	dehr ahn • dehnk • uhn • lah • duhn
the supermarket	**der Supermarkt**
	dehr zoo • pehr • mahrkt
the tobacconist	**der Tabakladen**
	dehr tah • bahk • lahd • uhn
the toy store	**das Spielzeuggeschäft**
	peel • tsoyg • geh • shehft

ASK AN ASSISTANT

When do you open/close?	**Wann öffnen/schließen Sie?**
	vahn erf • nuhn/shlees • uhn zee
Where's …?	**Wo ist …?**
	voh ihst …
the cashier	**die Kasse**
	dee kah • suh
the escalator	**die Rolltreppe**
	dee rohl • trehp • uh
the elevator [lift]	**der Fahrstuhl**
	dehr fahr • shtool
the fitting room	**die Umkleidekabine**
	dee oom • klied • uh • kah • bee • nuh
the store directory	**die Liste mit den Geschäften?**
	dee lihs • tuh miht dehn guh • sheft • tuhn
Can you help me?	**Können Sie mir helfen?**
	kern • uhn zee meer hehl • fuhn
I'm just looking.	**Ich schaue mich nur um.**
	eekh show • uh meekh noor oom
I'm already being helped.	**Ich werde schon bedient.**
	eekh vehrd • uh shohn buh • deent
Do you have …?	**Haben Sie …?**
	hah • buhn zee …

💬

YOU MAY HEAR...

Kann ich Ihnen helfen?
kahn eekh eehn • uhn hehlf • uhn

Can I help you?

Einen Moment.
ien • uhn moh • mehnt

One moment.

Was möchten Sie?
vahs merkht • uhn zee

What would you like?

Noch etwas?
nohkh eht • vahs

Anything else?

Can you show me...?	**Können Sie mir ... zeigen?** *kern • nuhn zee meer ... tsieg • uhn*
Can you ship/wrap it?	**Können Sie das versenden/einpacken?** *kern • uhn zee dahs fehr • zehn • duhn/ien • pahk • uhn*
How much?	**Wie viel kostet es?** *vee feel kohs • tuht ehs*
That's all.	**Das ist alles.** *dahs ihst ahl • uhs*

For Clothing, see page 117.

PERSONAL PREFERENCES

I'd like something...	**Ich möchte etwas ...** *eekh merkht • uh eht • vahs ...*
cheap/expensive	**Billiges/Teueres** *bihl • ee • guhs/toy • ehr • uhs*
larger/smaller	**Größeres/Kleineres** *grers • eh • ruhs/klien • eh • ruhs*
nicer	**Schöneres** *shern • uh • ruhs*

YOU MAY SEE...

GEÖFFNET/GESCHLOSSEN	open/closed
ÜBER MITTAG GESCHLOSSEN	closed for lunch
EINGANG	entrance
UMKLEIDEKABINE	fitting room
KASSE	cashier
NUR BARZAHLUNG MÖGLICH	cash only
KREDITKARTENZAHLUNG MÖGLICH	credit cards accepted
ÖFFNUNGSZEITEN	business hours
AUSGANG	exit

from this region	**aus dieser Region**	
	ows <u>deez</u> • ehr rehg • <u>yohn</u>	
Around...euros.	**Ungefähr ... Euro.**	
	<u>oon</u> • guh • fehr ... <u>oy</u> • roh	
Can you show me...?	**Können Sie mir ... zeigen?**	
	<u>kern</u> • uhn zee meer ... <u>tsieg</u> • uhn	
Is it real?	**Ist das echt?**	
	ihst dahs ehkht	
That's not quite what I want.	**Das ist nicht ganz das, was ich möchte.**	
	dahs ihst neekht gahnts dahs vahs eekh <u>merkht</u> • uh	
No, I don't like it.	**Das gefällt mir nicht.**	
	dahs guh • <u>fehlt</u> meer neekht	
It's too expensive.	**Es ist zu teuer.**	
	ehs ihst tsoo <u>toy</u> • ehr	
I have to think about it.	**Das muss ich mir überlegen.**	
	dahs moos eekh meer <u>ewb</u> • ehr • leh • guhn	
I'll take it.	**Ich nehme es.**	
	eekh <u>nehm</u> • uh ehs	

PAYING & BARGAINING

How much?	**Wie viel kostet es?**
	vee feel kohs • tuht ehs
I'll pay…	**Ich zahle …**
	eekh tsah • luh …
in cash	**bar**
	bahr
by credit card	**mit Kreditkarte**
	miht kreh • deet • kahr • tuh
by traveler's cheque	**mit Reiseschecks**
	miht riez • uh • shehks
A receipt, please.	**Die Quittung, bitte.**
	dee kviht • oong biht • tuh
That's too much.	**Das ist zu viel.**
	dahs ihst tsoo veel
I'll give you…	**Ich gebe Ihnen …**
	eekh gehb • uh eehn • uhn …
I have only… euros.	**Ich habe nur … Euro.**
	eekh hah • buh noor … oy • roh

In Germany, cash is the preferred form of payment. Credit cards are accepted in most larger stores, gas stations, hotels and restaurants. Credit cards may not be accepted by smaller businesses, so be sure to ask before making a purchase. Traveler's checks are not very popular in Germany. If taken, they should be exchanged for cash at a currency exchange office or bank, though a fee will be charged for the exchange. Some banks do not accept traveler's checks.

Is that your best price?	**Ist das Ihr bester Preis?**
	ihst dahs eehr behst • ehr pries

| Can you give me a discount? | **Können Sie mir einen Rabatt geben?** |
| | _kern • uhn zee meer ien • uhn rah • baht geh • buhn_ |

For Numbers, see page 22.

MAKING A COMPLAINT

I'd like...	**Ich möchte ...**
	eekh merkht • uh ...
to exchange this	**das umtauschen**
	dahs oom • tow • shuhn
a refund	**gern mein Geld zurück**
	gehrn mien gehld tsoo • rewk
to see the manager	**mit dem Manager sprechen**
	miht dehm mahn • ah • jehr shprehkh • uhn

SERVICES

Can you recommend...?	**Können Sie ... empfehlen?**
	kern • uhn zee ... ehm • pfeh • luhn
a barber	**einen Herrenfriseur**
	ien • uhn hehr • uhn • frih • zer

YOU MAY HEAR...

Wie möchten Sie zahlen?
vee merkht • uhn zee tsahl • uhn
How are you paying?

Ihre Kreditkarte wurde abgelehnt.
eehr • uh kreh • deet • kahr • tuh voor • duh ahp • guh • lehnt
Your credit card has been declined.

Ihren Ausweis, bitte.
eehr • uhn ows • vies biht • tuh
ID, please.

Wir nehmen keine Kreditkarten.
veer neh • muhn kie • nuh kreh • deet • kahr • tuhn
We don't accept credit cards.

Bitte nur Bargeld.
biht • tuh noor bahr • gehlt
Cash only, please.

Haben Sie Wechselgeld/kleine Scheine?
hah • buhn zee vehkh • zuhl • gehlt/ klien • uh shien • uh
Do you have change/small bills [notes]?

a dry cleaner	**eine Reinigung**
	ien • uh rien • ee • goong
a hairstylist	**einen Friseur**
	ien • uhn frih • zer
a laundromat [launderette]	**einen Waschsalon**
	ien • uhn vahsh • zah • lohn
a nail salon	**ein Nagelstudio**
	ien nah • gehl • shtood • yoh
a spa	**ein Wellness-Center**
	ien vehl • nuhs • sehn • tehr
a travel agency	**ein Reisebüro**
	ien rie • zuh • bew • roh
Can you...this?	**Können Sie das ...?**
	kern • uhn zee dahs ...

alter	**ändern**
	ehn • dehrn
clean	**reinigen**
	rien • ee • guhn
fix	**reparieren**
	reh • pah • reer • uhn
press	**bügeln**
	bewg • uhln
When will it be ready?	**Wann wird es fertig sein?**
	vahn veerd ehs fehr • teekh zien

HAIR & BEAUTY

I'd like...	**Ich möchte ...**
	eekh merkht • uh ...
an appointment for today/tomorrow	**einen Termin für heute/morgen**
	ien • uhn tehr • meen fewr hoy • tuh/ mohr • guhn
some color/ highlights	**die Haare/Strähnchen gefärbt bekommen**
	dee hah • ruh/shtrehnkh • uhn guh • ferbt buh • kohm • uhn
my hair styled/ blow-dried	**mein Haar stylen/fönen lassen**
	mien hahr shtew • luhn/fern • uhn lahs • uhn
a haircut	**einen Haarschnitt**
	ien • uhn hahr • shniht
an eyebrow/bikini wax	**eine Haarentfernung an den Augenbrauen/der Bikinizone**
	ien • uh hahr • ehnt • fehr • noong ahn dehn ow • guhn • brow • uhn/dehr bee • kee • nee • tsoh • nuh
a facial	**eine Gesichtsbehandlung**
	ien • uh guh • zeekhts • beh • hahnd • loong

a manicure/ pedicure	**eine Maniküre/Pediküre**
	ien • _uh_ mahn • eh • kewruh/
	pede • eh • kewruh
a (sports) massage	**eine (Sport-)Massage**
	ien • uh (shport-) mah • _sahdj_ • uh
a trim	**die Haare nachschneiden lassen**
	dee _hahr_ • uh _nahkh_ • shnayd • uhn
	lahs • uhn
Not too short.	**Nicht zu kurz.**
	neekht tsoo koorts
Shorter here.	**Hier kürzer.**
	heer _kewrts_ • ehr
Do you offer...?	**Machen Sie ...?**
	mahk • uhn zee ...
acupuncture	**Akupunktur**
	ah • koo • poonk • _toor_
aromatherapy	**Aromatherapie**
	ah • roh • mah • teh • _rah_ • pee
oxygen treatment	**Sauerstoffbehandlung**
	zow • ehr • shtohf • beh • hahnd • loong
Do you have a sauna?	**Haben Sie eine Sauna?**
	hah • buhn zee _ien_ • uh _zown_ • ah

ⓘ

Health resorts, day spas and hotel spas are popular destinations, and there are hundreds throughout Germany. Most spa towns have the word **Bad** in their names, for example: Bad Reichenhall, Europe's largest saline source, in Bavaria; Baden-Baden, considered the best and most fashionable; Wiesbaden, one of Germany's oldest cities and considered second best only to Baden-Baden; Bad Homburg, at the foot of Taunus Hills, once the summer retreat of Prussian kings; and Bad Nauheim, famous because both William Randolph Hearst and Elvis Presley were once guests experiencing the healing powers of the carbonic acid springs. Tipping varies by spa; ask about the tipping policy when booking or upon arrival.

ANTIQUES

How old is it?	**Wie alt ist es?**
	vee ahlt ihst ehs
Do you have anything from the… period?	**Haben Sie etwas aus der … Zeit?**
	hah • buhn zee eht • vahs ows dehr … tsiet
Do I have to fill out any forms?	**Muss ich irgendwelche Formulare ausfüllen?**
	moos eekh eer • guhnd • vehlkh • uh fohr • moo • lahr • uh ows • fewl • uhn
Is there a certificate of authenticity?	**Gibt es ein Echtheitszeugnis?**
	gihpt ehs ien ehkht • hiets • tsoyg • nuhs
Can you ship/wrap it?	**Können Sie es liefern/einpacken?**
	ker • nuhn zee ehs lee • fuhrn/ien • pahk • kuhn

CLOTHING

I'd like…	**Ich möchte …** *eekh merkht • uh …*
Can I try this on?	**Kann ich das anprobieren?** *kahn eekh dahs ahn • proh • bee • ruhn*
It doesn't fit.	**Es passt nicht.** *ehs pahst neekht*
It's too…	**Es ist zu …** *ehs ihst tsoo …*
big/small	**groß/klein** *grohs/klien*
short/long	**kurz/lang** *koorts/lahng*
tight/loose	**eng/weit** *ehng/viet*
Do you have this in size…?	**Haben Sie das in der Größe … ?** *hah • buhn zee dahs ihn dehr grers • uh …*
Do you have this in a bigger/ smaller size?	**Haben Sie das in einer größeren/ kleineren Größe?** *hah • buhn zee dahs ihn ien • ehr grers • ehr • uhn/klien • uh • ruhn grers • uh*

For Numbers, see page 22.

YOU MAY SEE…

HERRENABTEILUNG	men's (department)
DAMENABTEILUNG	women's (department)
KINDERABTEILUNG	children's (department)

COLORS

I'd like something...	**Ich möchte etwas ...**
	eekh merkht • uh eht • vahs ...
beige	**Beiges**
	behdj • uhs
black	**Schwarzes**
	shvahrtz • uhs
blue	**Blaues**
	blow • uhs
brown	**Braunes**
	brown • uhs
green	**Grünes**
	grewn • uhs
gray	**Graues**
	grow • uhs
orange	**Oranges**
	oh • rahnj • uhs
pink	**Pinkes**
	peenk • uhs
purple	**Violettes**
	vee • oh • leht • uhs
red	**Rotes**
	roht • uhs
white	**Weißes**
	vies • uhs
yellow	**Gelbes**
	gehlb • uhs

CLOTHES & ACCESSORIES

| a backpack | **der Rucksack** |
| | *dehr rook • zahk* |

a belt	**der Gürtel**
	dehr <u>gewrt</u> • uhl
a bikini	**der Bikini**
	dehr bih • <u>kee</u> • nee
a blouse	**die Bluse**
	dee <u>bloo</u> • zuh
a bra	**der BH**
	dehr beh • <u>hah</u>
briefs [underpants]	**der Schlüpfer**
	dehr <u>shlewp</u> • fehr
panties	**die Unterhosen**
	dee oont • ehr • hoh • suhn
a coat	**der Mantel**
	dehr <u>mahnt</u> • ehl
a dress	**das Kleid**
	dahs klied
a hat	**der Hut**
	dehr hoot
a jacket	**die Jacke**
	dee <u>yah</u> • kuh
jeans	**die Jeans**
	dee djeens
pajamas	**der Schlafanzug**
	dehr <u>shlahf</u> • ahn • tsoog
pants [trousers]	**die Hose**
	dee <u>hohz</u> • uh
pantyhose [tights]	**die Strumpfhose**
	dee <u>shtroompf</u> • hoh • zuh
a purse [handbag]	**die Handtasche**
	dee <u>hahnd</u> • tahsh • uh
a raincoat	**der Regenmantel**
	dehr <u>rehg</u> • uhn • mahn • tuhl
a scarf	**der Schal**
	dehr shahl

a shirt	**das Hemd**
	dahs hehmt
shorts	**die kurze Hose**
	dee koortz • uh hohz • uh
a skirt	**der Rock**
	dehr rohk
socks	**die Socken**
	dee zohk • uhn
a suit	**der Anzug**
	dehr ahn • tsoog
sunglasses	**die Sonnenbrille**
	dee zohn • uhn • brihl • uh
a sweater	**der Pullover**
	dehr pool • oh • fehr
a sweatshirt	**das Sweatshirt**
	dahs sveht • shehrt
a swimsuit	**der Badeanzug**
	dehr bah • deh • ahn • tsoog
a T-shirt	**das T-Shirt**
	dahs tee • shert
a tie	**die Krawatte**
	dee krah • vah • tuh
underwear	**die Unterwäsche**
	dee oon • tehr • vehsh • uh

YOU MAY HEAR...

Das steht Ihnen gut.
dahs shteht eehn • uhn goot

That looks great on you.

Passt es?
pahst ehs

How does it fit?

Wir führen Ihre Größe nicht.
veer fewhr • uhn eehr • uh grers • uh neekht

We don't have your size.

FABRIC

I'd like...	**Ich möchte …**
	eekh merkht • uh …
cotton	**Baumwolle**
	bowm • vohl • uh
denim	**Denim**
	dehn • ihm
lace	**Spitze**
	shpihts • uh
leather	**Leder**
	lehd • ehr
linen	**Leinen**
	lien • uhn
silk	**Seide**
	zied • uh
wool	**Wolle**
	vohl • uh
Is it machine washable?	**Ist es waschmaschinenfest?**
	ihst ehs vahsh • mah • sheen • uhn • fehst

SHOES

I'd like...	**Ich möchte ...** *eekh merkht • uh ...*
high-heels/flats	**Schuhe mit Absatz/ohne Absatz** *shoo • uh miht ahp • zahts/ohn • uh* *ahb • zahts*
boots	**Stiefel** *shtee • fuhl*
loafers	**Slipper** *slihp • ehr*
sandals	**Sandalen** *zahn • dahl • uhn*
shoes	**Schuhe** *shoo • uh*
slippers	**Badelatschen** *bah • duh • lahtsh • uhn*
sneakers	**Turnschuhe** *toorn • shoo • huh*
In size...	**In der Größe ...** *ihn dehr grers • uh ...*

For Numbers, see page 22.

SIZES

small (S)	**klein** *klein*
medium (M)	**mittel** *miht • tuhl*
large (L)	**gross** *grohs*
extra large (XL)	**extra gross** *ehks • trah grohs*

petite	**die Kurzgröße**
	dee koorts • grer • suh
plus size	**die Übergröße**
	dee ew • buhr • grer • suh

In addition to small, medium and large, many clothing articles are labeled by continental size. As that size varies by manufacturer, be sure to try on any article before buying.

NEWSSTAND & TOBACCONIST

Do you sell English-language newspapers?	**Haben Sie englischsprachige Zeitungen?**
	hah • buhn zee
	ehng • leesh • shprah • khee • guh
	tsie • toong • uhn
I'd like…	**Ich möchte …**
	eekh merkht • uh …
candy [sweets]	**Süßigkeiten**
	zews • eekh • kiet • uhn
chewing gum	**Kaugummi**
	kow • goo • mee
a chocolate bar	**einen Schokoladenriegel**
	ien • uhn shoh • koh • lahd • uhn • ree • guhl
a cigar	**eine Zigarre**
	ien • uh tsee • gahr • uh
a pack/carton of	**eine Schachtel/Stange Zigaretten**
	ien • uh
cigarettes	*shahkht • uhl/shtahng • uh*
	tsee • gahr • eht • uhn
a lighter	**ein Feuerzeug**
	ien foy • ehr • tsoyg
a magazine	**eine Zeitschrift**
	ien • uh tsiet • shrihft

matches	**Streichhölzer**
	shtriekh • herlts • uhr
a newspaper	**eine Zeitung**
	ien • uh _tsie_ • toong
a pen	**einen Stift**
	ien • uhn shtihft
a postcard	**eine Postkarte**
	ien • uh _pohst_ • kahr • tuh
a road/town map of...	**eine Straßenkarte/einen Stadtplan vonen ...**
	ien • uh _shtrahsuhn_ • kahrt • uh/_ien_ • uhn _shtaht_ • plahn fohn
stamps	**Briefmarken**
	breef • mahrk • uhn

PHOTOGRAPHY

I'd like a/an... camera.	**Ich möchte eine ... Kamera.**
	eekh _merkht_ • uh ien • uh ... _kah_ • meh • ruh
automatic	**automatische**
	ow • toh • _maht_ • ihsh • uh
digital	**digitale**
	dihd • juh • tuhl
disposable	**Wegwerf-**
	vehk • vehrf-
I'd like...	**Ich möchte ...**
	eekh _merkht_ • uh ...
a battery	**eine Batterie**
	ien • uh bah • tuh • _ree_
digital prints	**digitale Ausdrucke**
	dihd • juh • tuhl _ows_ • drook • uh
a memory card	**eine Speicherkarte**
	ien • uh _shpie_ • khuhr • kahrt • uh

Can I print digital photos here?	**Kann ich hier Digitalfotos ausdrucken lassen?**

kahn eekh heer dihd • jih • tahl • foh • tohs ows • droo • kuhn lahs • uhn

SOUVENIRS

Can I see this/that?	**Kann ich das sehen?**

kahn eekh dahs zeh • uhn

It's in the window/ display case.	**Es ist im Schaufenster/in der Vitrine.**

ehs ihst ihm schow • fehn • stehr/ihn dehr vih • tree • nuh

I'd like...   **Ich möchte ...**
eekh merkht • uh ...

a battery   **eine Batterie**
ien • uh bah • tuh • ree

a bracelet   **ein Armband**
ien ahrm • bahnt

a brooch   **eine Brosche**
ien • uh brohsh • uh

a clock   **eine Uhr**
ien • uh oohr

earrings   **Ohrringe**
oh • reeng • uh

a necklace   **eine Kette**
ien • uh keht • uh

a ring   **einen Ring**
ien • uhn reeng

a watch   **eine Uhr**
ien • uh oohr

I'd like...   **Ich möchte ...**
eekh merkht • uh ...

a beer stein   **einen Bierkrug**
ien • uh beer • kroog

a bottle of wine	**eine Flasche Wein**
	ien • uh flahsh • uh vien
a box of	**eine Schachtel Pralinen**
chocolates	*ien • uh shahkht • uhl prah • lee • nuhn*
a doll	**eine Puppe**
	ien • uh poo • puh
a key ring	**ein Schlüsselring**
	ien shlews • uhl • reeng
a postcard	**eine Postkarte**
	ien • uh post • kahr • tuh
pottery	**Töpferwaren**
	terp • fuhr • vah • ruhn
a T-shirt	**ein T-Shirt**
	ien tee • shehrt
a toy	**ein Spielzeug**
	ien shpeel • tsoyg
copper	**Kupfer**
	koop • fehr
crystal	**Kristall**
	krihs • tahl
diamonds	**Diamanten**
	dee • ah • mahn • tuhn
white/yellow gold	**Weißgold/Gelbgold**
	vies • gohlt/gehlb • gohlt
pearls	**Perlen**
	pehr • luhn
pewter	**Zinn**
	tsihn
platinum	**Platin**
	plah • teen
sterling silver	**Sterlingsilber**
	shtehr • leeng • zihl • behr
Is this real?	**Ist das echt?**
	ihst dahs ehkht

Can you engrave it? **Können Sie etwas eingravieren?**
ker • _nuhn zee_ _eht_ • _vahs_
ien • _grah_ • _vee_ • _ruhn_

One of Germany's most famous products is the Black
Forest cuckoo clock. Though very expensive, these clocks
will last for generations if properly cared for. Another popular
and less expensive souvenir is a traditional German beer
stein. Collector beer steins are made from clay, glass or
pewter and can be brightly painted, with or without a lid
and engraved. Germany is also known for its toys: wooden
figurines, porcelain dolls and model trains. Other souvenirs
include: **lederhosen** (traditional German pants), lace and
porcelain.

SPORT & LEISURE

NEED TO KNOW

When's the game?	**Wann findet das Spiel statt?**
	vahn fihnd • uht dahs shpeel shtaht
Where's…?	**Wo ist … ?**
	voh ihst …
the beach	**der Strand**
	dehr shtrahnd
the park	**der Park**
	dehr pahrk
the pool	**der Pool**
	dehr pool
Is it safe to swim here?	**Kann man hier schwimmen?**
	kahn mahn heer shvihm • uhn
Can I hire golf clubs?	**Kann ich Golfschläger ausleihen?**
	kahn eekh gohlf • shlelig • ehr ows • lie • uhn
How much per hour?	**Wie viel kostet es pro Stunde?**
	vee feel kohs • tuht ehs proh shtoond • uh
How far is it to…?	**Wie weit ist es bis zum m /zur f …?**
	vee viet ihst ehs bihs tsoom /tsoor …
Show me on the map, please.	**Zeigen Sie es mir bitte auf dem Stadtplan.**
	tsieg • uhn zee ehs meer biht • tuh owf dehm shtaht • plahn

WATCHING SPORT

When's…?	**Wann findet … statt?**
	vahn <u>fihnd</u> • uht … shtaht
the baseball game	**das Baseballspiel**
	dahs <u>behs</u> • bahl • shpeel
the basketball game	**das Basketballspiel**
	dahs <u>bahs</u> • kuht • bahl • shpeel
the boxing match	**der Boxkampf**
	dehr <u>bohx</u> • kahmpf
the cricket match	**das Cricket-Turnier**
	dahs <u>krih</u> • kuht • toor • neer
the cycling race	**das Radrennen**
	dahs <u>rahd</u> • rehn • uhn
the golf tournament	**das Golfturnier**
	dahs <u>gohlf</u> • toor • neer
the soccer [football] game	**das Fußballspiel**
	dahs <u>foos</u> • bahl • shpeel
the tennis match	**das Tennismatch**
	dahs <u>tehn</u> • ihs • mahch
the volleyball game	**das Volleyballspiel**
	dahs <u>voh</u> • lee • bahl • shpeel
Who's playing?	**Wer spielt?**
	vehr shpeelt

Where's the racetrack/stadium?	**Wo ist die Rennbahn/das Stadion?** *voh ihst dee <u>rehn</u>•bahn/dahs <u>shtah</u>•dyohn*
Where can I place a bet?	**Wo kann ich eine Wette abschließen?** *voh kahn eekh <u>ien</u>•uh <u>veh</u>•tuh <u>ahp</u>•shlees•uhn*

For Tickets, see page 47.

i

Germany's most popular sport is **Fußball** (soccer); in fact, Germany has won the World Cup three times. Tennis is another popular sport; the German Tennis Federation boasts membership of more than one million. Other popular sports include biking, hiking, handball, basketball, volleyball, ice hockey, golf and horseback riding.
Casinos are found throughout Germany. The spa towns, in particular, are home to well-known casinos.

PLAYING SPORT

Where is/are…?	**Wo ist/sind …?** *voh ihst/zihnt …*
the golf course	**der Golfplatz** *dehr <u>gohlf</u>•plahts*
the gym	**die Sporthalle** *dee <u>shpohrt</u>•hah•luh*
the park	**der Park** *dehr pahrk*
the tennis courts	**die Tennisplätze** *dee <u>tehn</u>•ihs•pleht•suh*
How much per…?	**Wie viel kostet es pro …?** *vee feel <u>kohs</u>•tuht ehs proh …*

day	**Tag**
	tak
hour	**Stunde**
	shtoond • uh
game	**Spiel**
	shpeel
round	**Runde**
	roond • uh
Can I rent [hire]…?	**Kann ich … ausleihen?**
	kahn eekh … ows • lie • huhn
golf clubs	**Golfschläger**
	gohlf • shlehg • ehr
equipment	**eine Ausrüstung**
	ien • uh ows • rews • toong
a racket	**einen Schläger**
	ien • uhn shlehg • ehr

AT THE BEACH/POOL

Where's the beach/pool?	**Wo ist der Strand/Pool?**
	voh ihst dehr shtrahnt/pool
Is there a…?	**Gibt es einen …?**
	gihpt ehs ien • uhn …
kiddie pool	**Pool für Kinder**
	pool fewr kihnd • ehr
indoor/outdoor pool	**Hallenbad/Freibad**
	hahl • ehn • baht/frie • baht
lifeguard	**Rettungsschwimmer**
	reht • oongs • shvihm • ehr
Is it safe to swim/dive?	**Ist es sicher zu schwimmen/tauchen?**
	ihst ehs sihk • hehr tsoo shvihm • uhn/ towkh • uhn
Is it safe for children?	**Ist es kindgerecht?**
	ihst ehs kihnt • guh • rehkht

ⓘ

Germany's main beach areas are located along the
North Sea and Baltic Sea coasts. There are numerous types
of beaches in Germany, including family, adults-only and
nude beaches. A few of the more popular areas include
Sylt, known for its nude beaches; Büsum, an intimate small
town with calm North Sea waters; Helgoland, a Frisian
island in the North Sea; Heiligendamm, Germany's oldest
seaside resort; Heringsdorf, on the island of Usedom; and
Kühlungsborn and Warnemünde, located on the Baltic Sea.

I'd like to rent hire…	**Ich möchte gern … ausleihen.** *eekh merkht • uh gehrn … ows • lie • uhn*
a deck chair	**einen Liegestuhl** *ien • uhn leeg • uh • shtoohl*
diving equipment	**eine Tauchausrüstung** *ien • uh towkh • ows • rew • stoong*
a jet ski	**einen Jet Ski** *ien • uhn djeht skee*
a motorboat	**ein Motorboot** *ien moht • ohr • boht*
a rowboat	**ein Ruderboot** *ien rood • ehr • boht*
snorkeling equipment	**eine Schnorchelausrüstung** *ien • uh shnohr • khehl • ows • rew • stoong*
a surfboard	**ein Surfboard** *ien soorf • bohrd*
a towel	**ein Handtuch** *ien hahnd • tookh*
an umbrella	**einen Schirm** *ien • uhn sheerm*
water skis	**Wasserski** *vahs • ehr • shee*

a windsurfer	**ein Surfbrett**
	ien serf • breht
For...hours.	**Für ... Stunden.**
	fewr ... <u>shtoond</u> • uhn

WINTER SPORTS

A lift pass for a day/ five days, please.	**Einen Liftpass für einen Tag/fünf Tage, bitte.**
	<u>ien</u> • uhn <u>lihft</u> • pahs fewr <u>ien</u> • uhn tahk/ fewnf <u>tahg</u> • uh <u>biht</u> • tuh
I'd like to hire...	**Ich möchte gerne ... ausleihen.**
	eekh <u>merkht</u> • uh <u>gehr</u> • nuh ... <u>ows</u> • lie • uhn
boots	**Stiefel**
	<u>shteef</u> • uhl
a helmet	**einen Helm**
	<u>ien</u> • uhn hehlm
poles	**Stöcke**
	<u>shterk</u> • uh
skis	**Skier**
	skee • ehr
a snowboard	**ein Snowboard**
	ien <u>snohw</u> • bohrd

snowshoes	**Schneeschuhe**
	shneh • shoo • uh
These are too big/small.	**Diese sind zu groß/klein.**
	dee • zuh zihnt tsoo grohs/klien
Are there lessons?	**Kann man Stunden nehmen?**
	kahn mahn shtoond • uhn neh • muhn
I'm a beginner.	**Ich bin Anfänger.**
	eekh bihn ahn • fehng • ehr
I'm experienced.	**Ich bin erfahren.**
	eekh been ehr • fahr • uhn
A trail [piste] map, please.	**Bitte einen Pistenplan.**
	biht • tuh ien • uhn pees • tuhn • plahn

YOU MAY SEE...

SCHLEPPLIFT	drag lift
SEILBAHN	cable car
SESSELLIFT	chair lift
ANFÄNGER	novice
FORTGESCHRITTENE	intermediate
KÖNNER	expert
PISTE GESCHLOSSEN	trail [piste] closed

Winter offers plenty of opportunities for outdoor activity in Germany. Alpine skiing, snowboarding, cross-country skiing, ice skating, tobogganing and hiking are just some of the options available to winter travelers.

OUT IN THE COUNTRY

A map of…, please.	**Eine Karte …, bitte.**
	ien • uh <u>kahrt</u> • uh … <u>biht</u> • tuh
this region	**dieser Region**
	<u>deez</u> • uhr rehg • <u>yohn</u>
the walking routes	**mit Wanderrouten**
	miht <u>vahnd</u> • ehr • root • uhn
the bike routes	**mit Radrouten**
	miht <u>rahd</u> • root • uhn
the trails	**mit Wanderwegen**
	miht <u>vahnd</u> • ehr • veh • guhn
Is it…?	**Ist es …?**
	ihst ehs …
easy	**leicht**
	liekht
difficult	**schwierig**
	<u>shveer</u> • eeg
far	**weit**
	viet
steep	**steil**
	shtiel
How far is it to…?	**Wie weit ist es bis …?**
	vee viet ihst ehs bihs …

Show me on the map, please.	**Zeigen Sie es mir bitte auf der Karte.**
	tsieg • uhn zee ehs meer biht • tuh owf dehr kahrt • uh
I'm lost.	**Ich habe mich verlaufen.**
	eekh hahb • uh meekh fehr • lowf • uhn
Where's…?	**Wo ist …?**
	voh ihst …
the bridge	**die Brücke**
	dee brew • kuh
the cave	**die Höhle**
	dee her • luh
the canyon	**der Canyon**
	dehr kahn • yohn
the cliff	**die Klippe**
	dee klih • puh
the desert	**die Wüste?**
	dee vews • tuh
the farm	**der Bauernhof**
	dehr bow • ehrn • hohf
the field	**das Feld**
	dahs fehld
the forest	**der Wald**
	dehr vahld
the hill	**der Hügel**
	dehr hew • gehl
the lake	**der See**
	dehr zeh
the mountain	**der Berg**
	dehr behrg
the nature preserve	**das Naturschutzgebiet**
	dahs nah • toor • shoots • guh • beet
the viewpoint	**der Aussichtspunkt**
	dehr ows • seekhts • poonkt
the park	**der Park**
	dehr pahrk

the path	**der Pfad**
	dehr pfahd
the peak	**der Gipfel**
	dehr <u>gihp</u> • fuhl
the picnic area	**der Picknickplatz**
	dehr <u>pihk</u> • nihk • plahts
the pond	**der Teich**
	dehr tiekh
the ravine	**die Schlucht**
	dee shlookht
the river	**der Fluss**
	dehr floos
the sea	**das Meer**
	dahs mehr
the (hot) spring	**die (heiße) Quelle**
	dee (<u>hie</u> • suh) <u>kveh</u> • luh
the stream	**der Strom**
	dehr shtrom
the valley	**das Tal**
	dahs tahl
the village	**das Dorf**
	dahs dohrf
the vineyard	**das Weingut**
	dahs <u>vien</u> • goot
the waterfall	**der Wasserfall**
	dehr <u>vahs</u> • ehr • fahl

TRAVELING WITH CHILDREN

NEED TO KNOW

Is there a discount for kids?	**Gibt es Ermäßigung für Kinder?** *gihpt ehs ehr • meh • see • goong fewr kihn • dehr*
Can you recommend a babysitter?	**Können Sie einen Babysitter empfehlen?** *kern • uhn zee ien • uhn beh • bee • siht • ehr ehm • pfeh • luhn*
Do you have a child's seat/highchair?	**Haben Sie einen Kindersitz/Kinderstuhl?** *hah • buhn zee ien • uhn kihnd • ehr • zihts/kihnd • ehr • shtoohl*
Where can I change the baby?	**Wo kann ich das Baby wickeln?** *voh kahn eekh dahs beh • bee vihk • uhln*

OUT & ABOUT

Can you recommend something for kids?	**Können Sie etwas für Kinder empfehlen?**
	kern • uhn zee eht • vahs fewr kihnd • ehr ehm • pfeh • luhn
Where's...?	**Wo ist ...?**
	voh ihst ...
the amusement park	**der Vergnügungspark**
	dehr fehrg • new • goongs • pahrk
the arcade	**die Spielhalle?**
	dee shpeel • hah • luh
the kiddie [paddling] pool	**das Kinderbecken**
	dahs kihnd • ehr • beh • kuhn
the park	**der Park**
	dehr pahrk
the playground	**der Spielplatz**
	dehr shpeel • plats
the zoo	**der Zoo**
	dehr tsoh
Are kids allowed?	**Sind Kinder erlaubt?**
	zihnt kihnd • ehr ehr • lowbt

YOU MAY HEAR...

Wie süß!
vee zews
How cute!

Wie heißt er m/**sie** f**?**
vee hiest ehr/zee
What's his/her name?

Wie alt ist er m/**sie** f**?**
vee ahlt ihst ehr/zee
How old is he/she?

Is it safe for kids?	**Ist es für Kinder geeignet?**
	ihst ehs fewr <u>kihnd</u> • ehr guh • <u>ieg</u> • nuht
Is it suitable for... year olds?	**Ist es für ... Jahre alte Kinder geeignet?**
	ihst ehs fewr ... <u>yah</u> • ruh <u>ahlt</u> • uh <u>kihnd</u> • ehr guh • <u>ieg</u> • nuht

For Numbers, see page 22.

BABY ESSENTIALS

Do you have...?	**Haben Sie ...?**
	<u>hah</u> • buhn zee ...
a baby bottle	**eine Babyflasche**
	<u>ien</u> • uh beh • bee • <u>flahsh</u> • uh
baby food	**Babynahrung**
	<u>beh</u> • bee • nahr • oong
baby wipes	**feuchte Babytücher**
	foykh • tuh <u>beh</u> • bee • tewkh • ehr
a car seat	**einen Kindersitz**
	<u>ien</u> • uhn <u>kihnd</u> • ehr • zihts
a children's menu/ portion	**ein Kindermenü/eine Kinderportion**
	<u>ien</u> • uhn <u>kihnd</u> • ehr • meh • new/<u>ien</u> • uh <u>kihnd</u> • ehr • pohrtz • yohn • uhn
a child's seat/ highchair	**einen Kindersitz/Kinderstuhl**
	<u>ien</u> • uhn <u>kihnd</u> • ehr • zihts/ <u>kihnd</u> • ehr • shtoohl
a crib/cot	**ein Gitterbett/Kinderbett**
	ien <u>giht</u> • tehr • beht/<u>kihnd</u> • ehr • beht
diapers [nappies]	**Windeln**
	<u>vihnd</u> • uhln
formula [baby food]	**Babynahrung**
	<u>beh</u> • bee • nah • roong
a pacifier [dummy]	**einen Schnuller**
	<u>ien</u> • uhn <u>shnool</u> • ehr

a playpen	**einen Laufstall**
	ien • uhn lowf • shtahl
a stroller	**einen Kinderwagen**
	ien • uhn
[pushchair]	*kihnd • ehr • vahg • uhn*
Can I breastfeed the baby here?	**Kann ich das Baby hier stillen?**
	kahn eekh dahs beh • bee heer shtihl • uhn
Where can I breastfeed/change the baby?	**Wo kann ich das Baby stillen/wickeln?**
	voh kahn eekh dahs beh • bee shtihl • uhn/ vihk • uhln

For Dining with Children, see page 172.

BABYSITTING

Can you recommend a babysitter?	**Können Sie einen Babysitter empfehlen?**
	kern • uhn zee ien • uhn beh • bee • siht • ehr ehm • pfeh • luhn
What is the cost?	**Was sind die Kosten?**
	vahs zihnt dee kohs • tuhn
I'll be back by...	**Ich bin um ... zurück.**
	eekh been oom ... tsoo • rewk
If you need to contact me, call...	**Ich bin unter ... zu erreichen.**
	eekh been oont • ehr ... tsoo ehr • riekh • uhn

For Time, see page 25.

SAFE TRAVEL

EMERGENCIES

NEED TO KNOW

Help!	**Hilfe!**
	hihlf • uh
Go away!	**Gehen Sie weg!**
	geh • uhn zee vehk
Stop, thief!	**Haltet den Dieb!**
	hahlt • uht dehn deeb
Get a doctor!	**Holen Sie einen Arzt!**
	hohl • uhn zee ien • uhn ahrtst
Fire!	**Feuer!**
	foy • ehr
I'm lost.	**Ich habe mich verlaufen.**
	eekh hahb • uh meekh fehr • lowf • uhn
Can you help me?	**Können Sie mir helfen?**
	kern • uhn zee meer hehlf • uhn

YOU MAY HEAR...

Füllen Sie dieses Formular aus.
fewl • uhn zee deez • uhs
fohr • moo • lahr ows

Fill out this form.

Ihren Ausweis, bitte.
eehr • uhn ows • vies biht • tuh

Your ID, please.

Wann/Wo ist es passiert?
vahn/voh ihst ehs pah • seert

When/Where did it happen?

Wie sah er m/sie f aus?
vee zah ehr/zee ows

What does he/she look like?

POLICE

NEED TO KNOW

Call the police!	**Rufen Sie die Polizei!**
	roof • uhn zee dee poh • leet • _sie_
Where's the police station?	**Wo ist das Polizeirevier?**
	voh ihst dahs poh • leet • _sie_ • ruh • veer
There was an accident/attack.	**Es gab einen Unfall/Überfall.**
	ehs gahb _ien_ • uhn _oon_ • fahl/ _ewb_ • ehr • fahl
My child is missing.	**Mein Kind ist weg.**
	mien kihnt ihst vehk
I need an interpreter.	**Ich brauche einen Dolmetscher.**
	eekh _browkh_ • uh _ien_ • uhn _dohl_ • mech • ehr
I need to contact my lawyer/make a phone call.	**Ich muss mit meinem Anwalt sprechen/ telefonieren.**
	eekh moos miht _mien_ • uhm _ahn_ • vahlt _shpreh_ • khehn/tehl • eh • fohn _eer_ • uhn
I'm innocent.	**Ich bin unschuldig.**
	eekh bihn _oon_ • shoold • eekh

CRIME & LOST PROPERTY

I want to report...	**Ich möchte ... melden.**
	eekh _merkht_ • uh ... _mehld_ • uhn
a mugging	**einen Überfall**
	ien • uhn _ewb_ • ehr • fahl
a rape	**eine Vergewaltigung**
	ien • uh fehr • guh • _vahlt_ • ee • goong

🛈

In an emergency, dial: **110** for the police
112 for the fire brigade
115 for the ambulance

a theft	**einen Diebstahl**
	ien • uhn deeb • shtahl
I've been mugged	**Ich wurde überfallen**
	eekh voor • duh ewb • ehr • fahl • uhn
I've been robbed	**Ich wurde beraubt**
	eekh voor • duh beh • rowbt
I've lost…	**Ich habe … verloren.**
	eekh hahb • uh … fehr • lohr • uhn
…was stolen.	**… wurde gestohlen.**
	… voor • duh geh • shtohl • uhn
my backpack	**Mein Rucksack**
	mien rook • zahk
my bicycle	**Mein Fahrrad**
	mien fahr • ahd
my camera	**Meine Kamera**
	mien • uh kah • meh • rah
my (hire) car	**Mein Mietauto**
	mien meet • ow • toh
my computer	**Mein Computer**
	mien kohm • pjoo • tehr
my credit card	**Meine Kreditkarte**
	mien • uh kreh • deet • kahrt • uh
my jewelry	**Mein Schmuck**
	mien shmook
my money	**Mein Geld**
	mien gehlt
my passport	**Mein Reisepass**
	mien riez • uh • pahs

my purse [handbag]	**Meine Handtasche** _mien • uh hahnd • tahsh • uh_
my traveler's checks [cheques]	**Meine Reisechecks** _mien • uh riez • uh • shehks_
my wallet	**Meine Brieftasche** _mien • uh breef • tahsh • uh_
I need a police report.	**Ich brauche einen Polizeibericht.** _eekh browkh • uh ien • uhn poh • leet • sie • beh • reekht_
Where is the British/ American/Irish embassy?	**Wo ist die britische/amerikanische/ irische Botschaft?** _voh ihst dee brih • tih • shuh/ ah • meh • rih • kah • nih • shuh/ eer • ih • shuh boht • shaft_

HEALTH

NEED TO KNOW

I'm sick.	**Ich bin krank.** _eekh bihn krahnk_
I need an English-speaking doctor.	**Ich brauche einen englischsprechenden Arzt.** _eekh browkh • uh ien • uhn ehng • glihsh • shprehkh • ehnd • uhn ahrtst_
It hurts here.	**Es tut hier weh.** _ehs toot heer veh_
I have a stomach ache.	**Ich habe Magenschmerzen.** _eekh hahb • uh mahg • uhn • shmehrt • suhn_

FINDING A DOCTOR

Can you recommend a doctor/dentist?	**Können Sie einen Arzt/Zahnarzt empfehlen?**
	kern • uhn zee ien • uhn ahrtst/ tsahn • ahrtst ehm • pfeh • luhn
Can the doctor come here?	**Kann der Arzt herkommen?**
	kahn dehr ahrtst hehr • kohm • uhn
I need an English-speaking doctor.	**Ich brauche einen englischsprechenden Arzt.**
	eekh browkh • uh ien • uhn ehng • gleesh • shprehkh • ehnd • uhn ahrtst
What are the office hours?	**Wann sind die Sprechstunden?**
	vahn zihnt dee shprekh • shtoond • uhn
It's urgent.	**Es ist dringend.**
	ehs ihst dreeng • uhnt
I'd like an appointment for...	**Ich möchte einen Termin für ...**
	eekh merkht • uh ien • uhn tehr • meen fewr ...
today	**heute**
	hoy • tuh
tomorrow	**morgen**
	mohr • guhn
as soon as possible	**so bald wie möglich**
	zoh bahld vee merg • leekh

SYMPTOMS

I'm bleeding.	**Ich blute.**
	eekh bloot • uh
I'm constipated.	**Ich habe Verstopfung.**
	eekh hahb • uh fehr • shtohpf • oong

I'm dizzy.	**Mir ist schwindlig.**
	meer ihst shvihnd • leekh
I'm nauseous.	**Mir ist schlecht.**
	meer ihst shlehkht
I'm vomiting.	**Ich übergebe mich.**
	eekh ewb • ehr • gehb • uh meekh
It hurts here.	**Es tut hier weh.**
	ehs toot heer veh
I have…	**Ich habe …**
	eekh hahb • uh …
an allergic reaction	**eine allergische Reaktion**
	ien • uh ah • lehr • geesh • uh reh • ahk • syon
chest pain	**Brustschmerzen**
	broost • shmehrt • suhn
cramps	**Krämpfe**
	krehmp • fuh
diarrhea	**Durchfall**
	doorkh • fahl
an earache	**Ohrenschmerzen**
	oht • uhn • shmehrt • suhn
a fever	**Fieber**
	feeb • ehr
pain	**Schmerzen**
	shmehrt • suhn
a rash	**einen Ausschlag**
	ien • uhn ows • shlahg
a sprain	**eine Verstauchung**
	ien • uh fehr • shtowkh • oong
some swelling	**eine Schwellung**
	ien • uh shvehl • oong
a sore throat	**Halsschmerzen**
	hahls • shmehrt • suhn
a stomachache	**Magenschmerzen**
	mahg • uhn • shmehrt • suhn

YOU MAY HEAR...

Was stimmt nicht mit Ihnen?
vahs shtihmt miht <u>eehn</u> • uhn
What's wrong?

Wo tut es weh?
voh toot ehs veh
Where does it hurt?

Tut es hier weh?
toot ehs heer veh
Does it hurt here?

Nehmen Sie Medikamente?
<u>nehm</u> • uhn zee mehd • ee • kah • <u>mehnt</u> • uh
Are you on medication?

Sind Sie auf irgendetwas allergisch?
zihnt zee owf eer • guhnd • <u>eht</u> • vahs ah • <u>lehr</u> • geesh
Are you allergic to anything?

Öffnen Sie Ihren Mund.
<u>erf</u> • nuhn zee <u>eehr</u> • uhn moont
Open your mouth.

Tief einatmen.
teef ien • <u>aht</u> • muhn
Breathe deeply.

Bitte husten.
<u>biht</u> • tuh <u>hoos</u> • tuhn
Cough, please.

Gehen Sie ins Krankenhaus.
<u>geh</u> • uhn zee ihns <u>krahnk</u> • uhn • hows
Go to the hospital.

Es ist ...
ehs ihst ...
It's...

  gebrochen
  geh • <u>brohkh</u> • uhn
broken

  ansteckend
  <u>ahn</u> • shtehk • uhnt
contagious

  infiziert
  een • fee • <u>tseert</u>
infected

  verstaucht
  fehr • <u>shtowkht</u>
sprained

  nichts Ernstes
  neekhts <u>ehrnst</u> • uhs
nothing serious

sunstroke	**einen Sonnenstich**
	ien • uhn <u>zohn</u> • uhn • shteekh
I've been sick [ill] for...days.	**Ich bin seit ... Tagen krank.**
	eekh bihn ziet ... <u>tahg</u> • uhn krahnk

CONDITIONS

I'm...	**Ich bin ...**
	eekh bihn ...
anemic	**anämisch**
	ah • <u>nay</u> • meesh
asthmatic	**Asthmatiker**
	ahst • <u>maht</u> • eek • ehr
diabetic	**Diabetiker**
	dee • ah • <u>beht</u> • eek • her
epileptic	**Epileptiker/Epileptikerin**
	eh • pih • lehp • tih • kuhr/
	eh • pih • lehp • tih • kuh • rihn
I'm allergic to antibiotics/ penicillin.	**Ich bin allergisch auf Antibiotika/ Penicillin.**
	eekh bihn <u>ah</u> • lehrg • eesh owf
	ahn • tee • bee • <u>oh</u> • tee • kah/
	peh • nih • <u>sihl</u> • ihn
I have...	**Ich habe ...**
	eekh <u>hahb</u> • uh ...
arthritis	**Arthritis**
	<u>ahr</u> • tree • tihs
a heart condition	**eine Herzkrankheit**
	<u>ien</u> • uh hehrts • krahnk • hiet
high/low blood pressure	**hohen/niedrigen Blutdruck**
	<u>hoh</u> • uhn/<u>need</u> • ree • gehn <u>bloot</u> • drook
I'm on...	**Ich nehme ...**
	eekh <u>nehm</u> • uh ...

For Meals & Cooking, see page 175.

TREATMENT

Do I need a prescription/medicine?	**Brauche ich ein Rezept/Medikament?** _browkh • uh eekh ien reh • tsehpt/_ _mehd • ee • kah • mehnt_
Can you prescribe a generic drug? [unbranded medication]	**Können Sie ein ähnliches, günstiges Medikament verschreiben?** _kern • uhn zee_ _ien ehn • lee • khehs gewn • stee • guhs_ _meh • dee • kah • mehnt fehr • shrieb • uhn_
Where can I get it?	**Wo kann ich es bekommen?** _voh kahn eekh ehs buh • kohm • uhn_
Is this over the counter?	**Ist es rezeptfrei?** _ihst ehs reh • tsehpt • frie_

HOSPITAL

Notify my family, please.	**Bitte benachrichtigen Sie meine Familie.** _biht • tuh buh • nahkh • reekh • tih • guhn_ _zee mien • uh fah • mee • lee • uh_
I'm in pain.	**Ich habe Schmerzen.** _eekh hahb • uh shmehrt • suhn_
I need a doctor/nurse.	**Ich brauche einen Arzt/eine Schwester.** _eekh browkh • uh ien • uhn ahrtst/ien • uh_ _shvehs • tehr_
When are visiting hours?	**Wann ist die Besuchszeit?** _vahn ihst dee beh • zookhs • tsiet_
I'm visiting…	**Ich besuche …** _eekh beh • zookh • uh …_

DENTIST

I have…	**Ich habe …** _eekh hahb • uh …_

a broken tooth	**einen kaputten Zahn**
	ien • uhn kah • _poot_ • uhn tsahn
a lost filling	**eine Füllung verloren**
	ien • uh _fewl_ • oong fehr • _lohr_ • uhn
a toothache	**Zahnschmerzen**
	tsahn • shmehrts • uhn
Can you fix this denture?	**Können Sie diese Prothese reparieren?**
	kern • uhn zee _deez_ • uh proh • _teh_ • zuh reh • pah • _reer_ • uhn

For What to Take, see page 155.

GYNECOLOGIST

I have cramps/ a vaginal infection.	**Ich habe Krämpfe/eine Scheideninfektion.**
	eekh _hahb_ • uh _krehmp_ • fuh/ie • nuh _shnied_ • uhn • ihn • fehk • tyohn
I missed my period.	**Meine Periode ist ausgeblieben.**
	mien • uh pehr • _yoh_ • duh ihst _ows_ • geh • bleeb • uhn
I'm on the Pill.	**Ich nehme die Pille.**
	eekh _nehm_ • uh dee _pihl_ • uh
I'm (one/two/three/ four/five/six/seven/ eight/nine months) pregnant.	**Ich bin (im ersten/zweiten/dritten/ vierten/fünften/sechsten/siebten/ achten/neunten Monat) schwanger.**
	eekh bihn (ihm ehrs • thun/ tsvai • thun/ dree • thun/feer • thun/ewnf • thun/ sehks • thun/seeb • thun/ahkh • thun/ noyn • thun moh • naht) shvahn • guhr
I'm not pregnant.	**Ich bin nicht schwanger.**
	eekh bihn (neekht) _shvahng_ • ehr
My last period was...	**Meine letzte Periode war ...**
	mien • uh lehts • uh pehr • _yohd_ • uh vahr ...

OPTICIAN

I've lost…	**Ich habe … verloren.** *eekh hahb • uh … fehr • lohr • uhn*
a contact lens	**eine Kontaktlinse** *ien • uh kohn • tahkt • lihnz • uh*
my glasses	**meine Brille** *mien • uh brihl • uh*
a lens	**ein Brillenglas** *ien brihl • uhn • glahs*

PAYMENT & INSURANCE

How much?	**Wie viel kostet es?** *vee feel kohs • tuht ehs*
Can I pay by credit card?	**Kann ich mit Kreditkarte bezahlen?** *kahn eekh miht kreh • deet • kahr • tuh beht • sahl • uhn*
I have insurance.	**Ich bin versichert.** *eekh bihn fehr • zeekh • ehrt*
I need a receipt for my insurance.	**Ich brauche eine Quittung für meine Versicherung.** *eekh browkh • uh ien • uh kviht • oong fewr mien • uh fehr • zeekh • ehr • oong*

PHARMACY

NEED TO KNOW

Where's the pharmacy?	**Wo ist die Apotheke?** *voh ihst dee ah • poh • tehk • uh*
What time does it open/close?	**Wann öffnet/schließt sie?** *vahn erf • nuht/shleest zee*
What would you recommend for…?	**Was empfehlen Sie bei …?** *vahs ehm • pfeh • luhn zee bie …*
How much do I take?	**Wie viel muss ich einnehmen?** *vee feel moos eekh ei • nehm • uhn*

WHAT TO TAKE

How much do I take?	**Wie viel muss ich einnehmen?** *vee feel moos eekh ien • nehm • uhn*
How often?	**Wie oft?** *vee ohft*
Is it safe for children?	**Ist es für Kinder geeignet?** *ihst ehs fewr kihnd • ehr geh • ieg • nuht*
I'm taking…	**Ich nehme …** *eekh neh • muh …*
Are there side effects?	**Gibt es Nebenwirkungen?** *gihpt ehs nehb • uhn • veerk • oong • uhn*
I need something for…	**Ich brauche etwas gegen …** *ihkh browkh • uh eht • vahs geh • guhn …*
a cold	**eine Erkältung** *ien • uh ehr • kehlt • oong*
a cough	**Husten** *hoos • tuhn*

diarrhea	**Durchfall**
	doorkh • fahl
a headache	**Kopfschmerzen**
	kohpf • shmehr • tsuhn
insect bites	**Insektenstiche**
	een • zehkt • uhn • shteekh • uh
motion [travel] sickness	**die Reisekrankheit**
	dee riez • uh • krahnk • hiet
a sore throat	**Halsschmerzen**
	hahls • shmehrt • suhn
sunburn	**Sonnenbrand**
	zohn • uhn • brahnt
a toothache	**Zahnschmerzen**
	tsahn • shmehr • tsuhn
an upset stomach	**eine Magenverstimmung**
	ien • uh mahg • uhn • fehr • shtihm • oong

💬

YOU MAY HEAR...

EINMAL/DREIMAL AM TAG	once/three times a day
TABLETTE	tablet
TROPFEN	drop
TEELÖFFEL	teaspoon
NACH/VOR/MIT DEN MAHLZEITEN	after/before/with meals
AUF LEEREN MAGEN	on an empty stomach
IM GANZEN SCHLUCKEN	swallow whole
KANN BENOMMENHEIT VERURSACHEN	may cause drowsiness
NUR ZÜR ÄUSSEREN ANWENDUNG	for external use only

In Germany, there is a distinction between **Apotheke** (pharmacy) and **Drogerie** (drugstore). **Die Apotheke**, usually featuring a large red A sign, dispenses prescription and over-the-counter medication. **Die Drogerie** sells toiletries and other personal items. Pharmacies are open 9:00 a.m. to 6:30 p.m. Monday to Friday, and from 9:00 a.m. to 1:00 p.m. (sometimes 4:00 p.m) on Saturday. Most large cities and towns have at least one 24-hour pharmacy. Closed pharmacies will have a sign on the door indicating the nearest 24-hour location.

BASIC SUPPLIES

I'd like…	**Ich hätte gern …**
	eekh <u>heh</u> • tuh gehrn …
acetaminophen [paracetamol]	**Paracetamol**
	pah • rah • <u>seht</u> • ah • mohl
antiseptic cream	**eine antiseptische Creme**
	ahn • tee • <u>zehp</u> • tee • shuh krehm
aspirin	**Aspirin**
	ahs • pih • <u>reen</u>
bandages	**Pflaster**
	<u>pflahs</u> • tehr
a comb	**einen Kamm**
	<u>ien</u> • uhn kahm
condoms	**Kondome**
	kohn • <u>dohm</u> • uh
contact lens solution	**Kontaktlinsenlösung**
	kohn • <u>tahkt</u> • lehnz • uhn • lerz • oong
deodorant	**Deodorant**
	deh • oh • doh • <u>rahnt</u>

a hairbrush	**eine Haarbürste**
	ien • uh <u>hahr</u> • bewr • stuh
hairspray	**Haarspray**
	<u>hahr</u> • shpraye
ibuprofen	**Ibuprofen**
	ee • boo • proh • <u>fuhn</u>
insect repellent	**Insektenspray**
	ihn • <u>zehkt</u> • uhn • shpray
lotion	**Lotion**
	loht • <u>syohn</u>
a nail file	**eine Nagelfeile**
	ien • uh <u>nahg</u> • ehl • fie • luh
a (disposable) razor	**(Wegwerf-) Rasierer**
	<u>vehk</u> • vehrf rah • <u>zeer</u> • ehr
razor blades	**Rasierklingen**
	rah • <u>zeer</u> • kleeng • uhn
rubbing alcohol	**Franzbranntwein**
[surgical spirit]	*<u>frahnts</u> • brahnt • vien*
sanitary napkins	**Monatsbinden**
[towels]	*<u>moh</u> • nahts • bihnd • uhn*
shampoo/	**Shampoo/Spülung**
conditioner	*<u>shahm</u> • poo/<u>shpewl</u> • oong*
soap	**Seife**
	<u>zie</u> • fuh
sunscreen	**Sonnenmilch**
	<u>zohn</u> • nuhn • mihlkh
tampons	**Tampons**
	<u>tahm</u> • pohns
tissues	**Taschentücher**
	<u>tahsh</u> • uhn • tewkh • ehr
toilet paper	**Toilettenpapier**
	toy • <u>leht</u> • uhn • pah • peer
toothpaste	**Zahnpasta**
	<u>tsahn</u> • pahs • tah

For Baby Essentials, see page 140.

CHILD HEALTH & EMERGENCY

Can you recommend a pediatrician?	**Können Sie einen Kinderarzt empfehlen?** *kern • uhn zee <u>ien</u> • uhn <u>kihnd</u> • ehr • ahrtst ehm • <u>pfeh</u> • luhn*
My child is allergic to…	**Mein Kind ist allergisch auf …** *mien kihnt ihst ah • <u>lehrg</u> • eesh owf …*
My child is missing.	**Mein Kind ist weg.** *mien kihnt ihst vehk*
Have you seen a boy/girl?	**Haben Sie einen Jungen/ein Mädchen gesehen?** *<u>hah</u> • buhn zee <u>ien</u> • uhn <u>yoong</u> • uhn/ien <u>meht</u> • khuhn guh • <u>zeh</u> • uhn*

For Police, see page 145.

DISABLED TRAVELERS

NEED TO KNOW

Is there…?	**Gibt es …?**
	gihpt ehs …
access for the disabled	**einen Zugang für Behinderte**
	ien • uhn <u>tsoo</u> • gahng fewr beh • <u>hihnd</u> • ehrt • uh
a wheelchair ramp	**eine Rollstuhlrampe**
	ien • uh <u>rohl</u> • shtool • rahm • puh
a disabled-accessible toilet	**eine Behindertentoilette**
	ien • uh beh • <u>hihn</u> • dehrt • uhn • toy • leh • tuh
I need…	**Ich brauche …**
	eekh <u>browkh</u> • uh …
assistance	**Hilfe**
	hihlf • uh
an elevator [a lift]	**einen Fahrstuhl**
	ien • uhn <u>fahr</u> • shtoohl
a ground-floor room	**ein Zimmer im Erdgeschoss**
	ien <u>tsihm</u> • ehr ihm <u>ehrd</u> • guh • shohs

ASKING FOR ASSISTANCE

I'm…	**Ich bin …**
	eekh bihn …
disabled	**behindert**
	beh • <u>hihn</u> • dehrt
visually impaired	**sehbehindert**
	<u>zeh</u> • buh • hihn • dehrt

hearing impaired/	**hörgeschädigt/taub**
deaf	_her • guh • sheh • deegt/towb_
I'm unable to walk far/use the stairs.	**Ich kann nicht weit laufen/die Treppe benutzen.**
	eekh kahn neekht viet <u>low</u> • fuhn/dee <u>trehp</u> • uh beh • <u>noot</u> • suhn
Please speak louder.	**Bitte sprechen Sie lauter.**
	biht • tuh <u>shprehkh</u> • uhn zee <u>lowt</u> • ehr
Can I bring my wheelchair?	**Kann ich meinen Rollstuhl mitbringen?**
	kahn eekh <u>mien</u> • uhn <u>rohl</u> • shtoohl <u>miht</u> • brihng • uhn
Are guide dogs permitted?	**Sind Blindenhunde erlaubt?**
	zihnt <u>blihnd</u> • uhn • hoond • uh ehr • <u>lowbt</u>
Can you help me?	**Können Sie mir helfen?**
	kern • uhn zee meer <u>hehlf</u> • uhn
Please open/hold the door.	**Bitte öffnen/halten Sie die Tür.**
	biht • tuh <u>erf</u> • nuhn/<u>hahlt</u> • uhn zee dee tewr

For Health, see page 147.

FOOD

EATING OUT

NEED TO KNOW

Can you recommend a good restaurant/bar?
Können Sie ein gutes Restaurant/eine gute Bar empfehlen?
ker • nuhn zee ien <u>goo</u> • tuhs reh • stow • <u>rahnt</u>/<u>ien</u> • uh goo • tuh bahr ehm • <u>pfeh</u> • luhn

Is there a traditional German/an inexpensive restaurant nearby?
Gibt es in der Nähe ein typisch deutsches/preisgünstiges Restaurant?
gihpt ehs ihn dehr <u>neh</u> • uh ien <u>tew</u> • peesh doy • chuhs/<u>pries</u> • gewn • stee • guhs reh • stow • <u>rahnt</u>

A table for..., please.
Bitte einen Tisch für ...
<u>biht</u> • tuh <u>ien</u> • uhn tihsh fewr ...

Can we sit...?
Können wir ... sitzen?
<u>ker</u> • nuhn veer ... <u>ziht</u> • tsuhn

here/there
hier/dort
heer/dohrt

outside
draußen
<u>drow</u> • suhn

in a non-smoking area
in einem Nichtraucherbereich
ihn <u>ien</u> • uhm neekht • <u>row</u> • khehr • beh • riehk

I'm waiting for someone.
Ich warte auf jemanden.
eekh <u>vahr</u> • tuh owf <u>yeh</u> • mahnd • uhn

Where are the toilets?
Wo ist die Toilette?
voh ihst dee toy • <u>leh</u> • tuh

A menu, please.	**Die Speisekarte, bitte.**
	dee <u>shpie</u> • zuh • kahr • tuh <u>biht</u> • tuh
What do you recommend?	**Was empfehlen Sie?**
	vahs ehm • <u>pfeh</u> • luhn zee
I'd like…	**Ich möchte …**
	eekh <u>merkh</u> • tuh …
Some more…, please.	**Etwas mehr …, bitte.**
	<u>eht</u> • vahs mehr … <u>biht</u> • tuh
Enjoy your meal!	**Guten Appetit!**
	<u>goo</u> • tuhn ah • puh • <u>teet</u>
The check [bill], please.	**Die Rechnung, bitte.**
	dee <u>rehkh</u> • noonk <u>biht</u> • tuh
Is service included?	**Ist die Bedienung im Preis enthalten?**
	ihsht dee buh • <u>dee</u> • nung ihm pries ehnt • hahl • tuhn
Can I pay by credit card/have a receipt?	**Kann ich mit Kreditkarte bezahlen/ eine Quittung haben?**
	kahn eekh miht kreh • <u>deet</u> • kahr • tuh beht • <u>sahl</u> • uhn/ien • uh <u>kvee</u> • toonk <u>hah</u> • buhn
Thank you!	**Danke!**
	<u>dahn</u> • kuh

WHERE TO EAT

Can you recommend…?	**Können Sie … empfehlen?**
	<u>ker</u> • nuhn zee … ehm • <u>pfeh</u> • luhn
a restaurant	**ein Restaurant**
	ien reh • stow • <u>rahnt</u>
a bar	**eine Bar**
	<u>ien</u> • uh bahr

a cafe	**ein Café**
	ien kah • feh
a fast-food place	**ein Schnellrestaurant**
	ien shnehl • reh • stow • rahnt
a snack bar	**einen Imbiss**
	ien • uhn ihm • bees
a cheap restaurant	**ein billiges Restaurant**
	ien bihl • lee • guhs reh • stow • rahnt
an expensive restaurant	**ein teures Restaurant**
	ien toy • rehs reh • stow • rahnt
a restaurant with a good view	**ein Restaurant mit schöner Aussicht**
	ien reh • stow • rahnt miht sher • nuhr ows • seekht
an authentic/ a non-touristy restaurant	**ein authentisches/ein nicht so touristisches Restaurant**
	ien ow • tehn • tih • shuhs/ien neekht zoh tou • rihs • tih • shuhs reh • stow • rahnt

RESERVATIONS & PREFERENCES

I'd like to reserve a table...	**Ich möchte einen Tisch ... reservieren**
	eekh merkh • tuh ien • uhn tihsh ... reh • zuh • veer • ehn
for two	**für zwei Personen**
	fewr tsvie pehr • zohn • uhn
for this evening	**für heute Abend**
	fewr hoy • tuh ah • behnt
for tomorrow at...	**für morgen um ...**
	fewr mohr • guhn oom ...
A table for two, please.	**Bitte einen Tisch für zwei.**
	biht • tuh ien • uhn tihsh fewr tsvie
We have a reservation.	**Wir haben eine Reservierung.**
	veer hah • buhn ien • uh reh • zuh • veer • uhng

My name is…	**Mein Name ist …**
	mien <u>nahm</u> • uh ihst …
Can we sit…?	**Können wir … sitzen?**
	<u>ker</u> • nuhn veer … <u>ziht</u> • tsuhn
here/there	**hier/dort**
	heer/dohrt
outside	**draußen**
	<u>drow</u> • suhn
in a non-smoking area	**in einem Nichtraucherbereich**
	ihn <u>ien</u> • uhm
	<u>neekht</u> • row • khuhr • beh • riekh
by the window	**am Fenster**
	ahm <u>fehn</u> • stehr
in the shade	**im Schatten**
	ihm shaht • tehn

YOU MAY HEAR…

💬

Haben Sie eine Reservierung?	Do you have
<u>hah</u> • buhn zee <u>ien</u> • uh	a reservation?
reh • zuh • <u>veer</u> • uhng	
Für wie viele Personen?	For how many
fewr vee <u>fee</u> • luh pehr • <u>zohn</u> • uhn	people?
Raucher oder Nichtraucher?	Smoking or non-
<u>row</u> • khuhr oh • duhr <u>neekht</u> • row • khuhr	smoking?
Möchten Sie jetzt bestellen?	Are you ready to
<u>merkh</u> • tuhn zee yehtst buh • <u>shteh</u> • luhn	order?
Was möchten Sie?	What would you
vahs <u>merkh</u> • tuhn zee	like?
Ich empfehle …	I recommend…
eekh ehm • <u>pfeh</u> • luh …	
Guten Appetit.	Enjoy your meal.
<u>goo</u> • tuhn ah • puh • <u>teet</u>	

in the sun	**in der Sonne**
	ihn dehr sohn • nuh
Where are the toilets?	**Wo ist die Toilette?**
	voh ihst dee toy • leh • tuh

HOW TO ORDER

Waiter/Waitress!	**Bedienung!**
	buh • dee • nounk
We're ready to order.	**Wir möchten bitte bestellen.**
	weer merkh • tuhn biht • tuh
	buh • shteh • luhn
May I see the wine list, please?	**Die Weinkarte, bitte.**
	dee vien • kahr • tuh biht • tuh
I'd like…	**Ich möchte …**
	eekh merkh • tuh …
a bottle of…	**eine Flasche …**
	ien • uh flah • shuh …
a carafe of…	**eine Karaffe …**
	ien • uh kah • rah • fuh …
a glass of…	**ein Glas …**
	ien glahs …
The menu, please.	**Die Speisekarte, bitte.**
	dee shpie • zuh • kahr • tuh biht • tuh
Do you have…?	**Haben Sie …?**
	hah • buhn zee …
a menu in English	**eine Speisekarte in Englisch**
	ien • uh shpie • zuh • kahr • tuh ihn
	ehn • gleesh
a fixed-price menu	**ein Festpreismenü**
	ien fehst • pries • meh • new
a children's menu	**ein Kindermenü**
	ien kihn • dehr • meh • new
What do you recommend?	**Was empfehlen Sie?**
	vahs ehm • pfeh • luhn zee

What's this?	**Was ist das?**
	vahs ihsht dahs
What's in it?	**Was ist darin?**
	vahs ihsht dah • <u>rihn</u>
Is it spicy?	**Ist es scharf?**
	ihsht ehs shahrf
I'd like…	**Ich möchte gern …**
	eekh <u>merkh</u> • tuh gehrn …
More…, please.	**Mehr …, bitte.**
	mehr … <u>biht</u> • tuh
With/Without…	**Mit/Ohne …**
	miht/<u>oh</u> • nuh …
I can't eat…	**Ich vertrage kein/keine …**
	eekh fehr • <u>trah</u> • guh kien/<u>kien</u> • uh …
rare	**roh**
	roh
medium	**medium**
	<u>meh</u> • dee • uhm
well-done	**durchgebraten**
	<u>doorkh</u> • geh • brah • tuhn
Without…, please.	**Ohne …, bitte.**
	<u>oh</u> • nuh …<u>biht</u> • tuh
It's to go [take away], please.	**Bitte zum Mitnehmen.**
	<u>biht</u> • tuh tsoom <u>miht</u> • neh • muhn

For Drinks, see page 193.

YOU MAY SEE…

SPEISEKARTE	menu
TAGESMENÜ	menu of the day
SPEZIALITÄTEN	specials

COOKING METHODS

baked	**gebacken**
	guh • bahkh • uhn
boiled	**gekocht**
	guh • kohkht
braised	**geschmort**
	guh • shmohrt
breaded	**paniert**
	pah • neert
creamed	**püriert**
	pew • reert
diced	**gewürfelt**
	guh • vewr • fuhlt
filleted	**filetiert**
	fee • luh • teert
fried	**gebraten**
	guh • brah • tuhn
grilled	**gegrillt**
	guh • grihlt
poached	**pochiert**
	poh • sheert
roasted	**geröstet**
	guh • rer • stuht

sautéed	**sautiert**
	zow • teert
smoked	**geräuchert**
	guh • _roy_ • khuhrt
steamed	**gedünstet**
	guh • _dewn_ • stuht
stewed	**geschmort**
	guh • _shmohrt_
stuffed	**gefüllt**
	guh • _fewlt_

DIETARY REQUIREMENTS

I'm…	**Ich bin …**
	eekh bihn …
diabetic	**Diabetiker**
	dee • ah • _beh_ • tee • kehr
lactose intolerant	**laktoseintolerant**
	lahk • thoh • suh • een • tho • luh • rahnt
vegetarian	**Vegetarier**
	veh • guh • _tah_ • ree • ehr
vegan	**Veganer**
	veh • gah • nehr
I'm allergic to…	**Ich bin allergisch auf …**
	eekh bihn ah • _lehr_ • geesh owf …
I can't eat…	**Ich kann … essen.**
	eekh kahn … _eh_ • zuhn
dairy products	**keine Milchprodukte**
	kien • uh _meelkh_ • proh • dook • tuh
gluten	**kein Gluten**
	kien _gloo_ • tuhn
nuts	**keine Nüsse**
	kien • uh _new_ • suh
pork	**kein Schweinefleisch**
	kien _shvie_ • nuh • fliesh

shellfish	**keine Schalentiere**	
	kien • _uh_ _shah_ • luhn • tee • ruh	
spicy foods	**keine scharf gewürzten Speisen**	
	kien • _uh_ shahrf guh • _vewrt_ • stuhn shpie • zuhn	
wheat	**kein Weizen**	
	kien _vie_ • tsuhn	
Is it halal/kosher?	**Ist es halal/koscher?**	
	ihsht ehs hah • _lahl/koh_ • shuhr	
Do you have...?	**Haben Sie...?**	
	hah • buhn zee	
skimmed milk	**Magermilch**	
	mah • _guhr_ • meelkh	
whole milk	**Vollmilch**	
	foll • meelkh	
soya milk	**Sojamilch**	
	soh • yah • meelkh	

DINING WITH CHILDREN

Do you have children's portions?	**Haben Sie Kinderportionen?** _hah_ • buhn zee _kihn_ • dehr • pohr • syoh • nuhn	
Can I have a highchair/ child's seat?	**Einen Kindersitz/Kinderstuhl, bitte.** _ien_ • uhn _kihnd_ • ehr • zihtz/ _kihn_ • dehr • shtuhl _biht_ • tuh	
Where can I feed/ change the baby?	**Wo kann ich das Baby füttern/wickeln?** voh kahn eekh dahs _beh_ • bee few • tuhrn/ _vihk_ • uhln	
Can you warm this?	**Können Sie das warm machen?** _ker_ • nuhn zee dahs vahrm _mah_ • khuhn	

For Traveling with Children, see page 138.

HOW TO COMPLAIN

When will our food be ready?	**Wie lange dauert es noch mit dem Essen?** *vee lahng • uh dow • ehrt ehs nohkh miht dehm eh • suhn*
We can't wait any longer.	**Wir können nicht mehr länger warten.** *veer ker • nuhn neekht mehr lehng • ehr vahr • tuhn*
We're leaving.	**Wir gehen jetzt.** *veer geh • ehn yehtst*
I didn't order this.	**Das habe ich nicht bestellt.** *dahs hah • buh eekh neekht buh • shtehlt*
I ordered…	**Ich habe … bestellt.** *eekh hah • buh … buh • shtehlt*
I can't eat this.	**Ich kann das nicht essen.** *eekh kahn dahs neekht eh • suhn*
This is too…	**Das ist zu …** *dahs ihsht tsoo …*
cold/hot	**kalt/heiß** *kahlt/hies*
salty/spicy	**salzig/scharf gewürzt** *sahl • tseek/shahrf guh • vewrts*
tough/bland	**zäh/fad** *tseh/fahd*
This isn't clean/fresh.	**Das ist nicht sauber/frisch.** *dahs ihsht neekht zow • buhr/frihsh*

Service is included in the bill in German restaurants and bars, as is value added tax (VAT). However, it is still typical to give a small tip, rounding up to the nearest euro or two for a small bill or adding 5-10% for a bigger bill. Note that it is not usual to be given an actual check [bill]. Instead, the server will just tell you what your total is and you hand them the money, specifying how much change you would like to have back, allowing for the tip you want to give.

PAYING

The check [bill], please.
Die Rechnung, bitte.
dee rehkh • noonk biht • tuh

Separate checks [bills], please.
Getrennte Rechnungen, bitte.
geh • trehn • tuh rehkh • noong • uhn biht • tuh

It's all together.
Alles zusammen.
ah • luhs tsoo • zah • muhn

Is service included?
Ist die Bedienung im Preis enthalten?
ihsht dee buh • dee • noonk ihm pries ehnt • hahl • tuhn

What's this amount for?
Wofür ist diese Summe?
voh • fewr ihsht dee • zuh soo • muh

I didn't have that. I had…
Das hatte ich nicht. Ich hatte …
dahs hah • tuh eekh neekht eekh hah • tuh …

Can I…?
Kann ich …?
kahn eekh …

pay with a credit card
mit Kreditkarte bezahlen
miht kreh • deet • kahr • tuh beht • sahl • uhn

have a receipt
eine Quittung haben
ien • uh kvee • toonk hah • buhn

have an itemized bill	**eine aufgeschlüsselte Rechnung haben**
	ien • _uh_ _owf_ • _guh_ • _shlew_ • _sehl_ • _tuh_
	rehkh • _oong_ • _uhn_ _hah_ • _buhn_
That was delicious!	**Das war lecker!**
	dahs vahr leh • _khehr_
I've already paid.	**Ich habe schon bezahlt.**
	eekh hah • _buh shohn beht_ • _sahlt_

MEALS & COOKING

BREAKFAST

der Apfelsaft	apple juice
dehr ah • _pfuhl_ • _zahft_	
der Aufschnitt	cold cuts
dehr owf • _shniht_	[charcuterie]
das Brot	bread
dahs broht	
das Brötchen	roll
dahs brert • _khuhn_	
die Butter	butter
dee boo • _tehr_	
das ... Ei	...egg
dahs ... ie	
hart/weich gekochte	hard-/soft-boiled
hahrt/viekh guh • _kohkh_ • _tuh_	
der Joghurt	yogurt
dehr yoh • _goort_	
der Kaffee/Tee ...	coffee/tea...
dehr kah • _feh_/tee ...	
entkoffeiniert	decaf
ehnt • _koh_ • _feh_ • _een_ • _eert_	

mit Milch *miht mihlkh*	with milk
mit Süßstoff *miht <u>zews</u> • shtohf*	with artificial sweetener
mit Zucker *miht <u>tsoo</u> • khuhr*	with sugar
schwarz *shvahrts*	black
der Käse *dehr <u>kay</u> • zuh*	cheese
der Kräutertee *dehr <u>krow</u> • tehr • tee*	herbal tea
die Marmelade *dee mahr • muh • <u>lah</u> • duh*	jam/jelly
die Milch *dee mihlkh*	milk
der Muffin *dehr <u>moo</u> • fihn*	muffin
das Müsli *dahs <u>mew</u> • slee*	granola [muesli]
das Omelett *dahs <u>ohm</u> • luht*	omelet

Das Frühstück (breakfast) can range from a large meal, usually served buffet style, to a simple dish of bread, jam and butter. **Das Mittagessen** (lunch), typically a large and heavy meal, is normally served from 12:00 to 2:00 p.m. In larger cities, many Germans will have lunch at a beer garden or hall with cafeteria-style service. **Das Abendessen** (dinner) is served from 6:00 to 9:00 p.m. and is usually a light meal.

der Orangensaft   orange juice
dehr oh • rahng • uhn • zahft
der Pampelmusensaft   grapefruit juice
dehr pahm • puhl • moo • zuhn • zahft
das Rührei   scrambled egg
dahs rew • rie
der Saft   juice
dehr zahft
der Schinken   ham
dehr shihn • kuhn
das Spiegelei   fried egg
dahs shpeeg • uh • lie
der Toast   toast
dehr tohst
das Wasser   water
dahs vah • sehr

APPETIZERS

die Appetithäppchen   finger sandwiches
dee ah • peh • teet • hehp • khehn
die Aufschnittplatte   cold cuts served with
dee owf • shniht • plah • tuh   bread

der Bismarckhering marinated herring
dehr bees • mahrk • heh • reeng with onions

die Fleischpastete meat pâté
dee fliesh • pah • steh • tuh

die Gänseleberpastete goose liver pâté
dee gehn • zehl • leh • behr • pah • steh • tuh

die gefüllten Champignons stuffed mushrooms
dee geh • fewl • tehn shahm • pee • nyohns

der gemischte Salat mixed salad
dehr geh • meesh • tuh sah • laht

die Käseplatte cheese platter
dee kay • zuh • plah • tuh

das Knoblauchbrot garlic bread
dahs knoh • blowkh • broht

der Krabbencocktail shrimp cocktail
dehr krahb • behn • kohk • tayl

die russischen Eier hard-boiled eggs
dee roo • see • shuh ier with mayonnaise

der Räucherlachs smoked salmon
dehr roy • khurt • lahks

der Salat salad
dehr sah • laht

die Soleier eggs boiled in brine
dee soh • lier

der Tomatensalat tomato salad
dehr toh • mah • tehn • sah • laht

der Wurstsalat cold cuts with onion
dehr voorst • sah • laht and oil

SOUP

die Backerbsensuppe broth with crisp,
dee bahk • ehrb • sehn • zoo • puh round noodles

die Bohnensuppe bean soup
dee boh • nuhn • zoo • puh

die Champignoncremesuppe — cream of mushroom soup
dee shahm • pee • nyohn • krehm • zoo • puh

die Erbsensuppe — pea soup
dee ehrb • zuhn • zoo • puh

die Fleischbrühe — bouillon
dee fliesh • brew • uh

die Frittatensuppe — broth with pancake strips
dee free • tah • tehn • zoo • puh

die Frühlingssuppe — spring vegetable soup
dee frew • leeng • zoo • puh

die Gemüsesuppe — vegetable soup
dee guh • mew • zuh • zoo • puh

die Gulaschsuppe — stewed beef in a spicy soup
dee gool • ahsh • zoo • puh

die Hühnersuppe — chicken soup
dee hewn • ehr • zoo • puh

die klare Gemüsebrühe — vegetable broth
dee klah • ruh geh • mew • zuh • brew • uh

die Linsensuppe — lentil soup
dee leen • zehn • zoo • puh

die Semmelknödelsuppe — bread dumpling soup
dee zeh • mehl • kner • dehl • zoo • puh

die Tomatensuppe — tomato soup
dee toh • mah • tuhn • zoo • puh

die Zwiebelsuppe — onion soup
dee tsvee • behl • zoo • puh

FISH & SEAFOOD

der Aal — eel
dehr ahl

die Auster — oyster
dee ow • stehr

die Brachse — bream
dee brahk • suh

der Barsch	perch
dehr bahrsh	
der Brathering	fried sour herring
dehr <u>brah</u> • theh • reeng	
der Dorsch	cod
dehr dohrsh	
die Forelle	trout
dee foh • <u>reh</u> • luh	
die Garnele	shrimp
dee gahr • <u>neh</u> • luh	
der Heilbutt	halibut
dehr <u>hiel</u> • boot	
der Hering	herring
dehr <u>heh</u> • rihng	
der Hummer	lobster
dehr <u>hoo</u> • mehr	
der Krebs	crab
dehr krehbs	
der Lachs	salmon
dehr lahks	
die Makrele	mackerel
dee <u>mah</u> • kreh • luh	
die Muschel	clam
dee <u>moo</u> • shuhl	

der Oktopus
dehr <u>ohk</u> • toh • poos
octopus

die Sardelle
dee sahr • <u>deh</u> • luh
anchovy

die Sardine
dee zahr • <u>dee</u> • nuh
sardine

die Scholle
dee <u>shoh</u> • luh
flounder

der Schwertfisch
dehr <u>shvehrt</u> • fihsh
swordfish

der Seebarsch
dehr <u>zeh</u> • bahrsh
sea bass

die Seezunge
dee <u>zeh</u> • tsoong • uh
sole

der Tintenfisch
dehr <u>tihn</u> • tuhn • fihsh
squid

der Thunfisch
dehr <u>toon</u> • fihsh
tuna

MEAT & POULTRY

die Berliner Buletten
dee behr • <u>lee</u> • nuh boo • <u>leh</u> • tehn
fried meatballs, a specialty of Berlin

der Braten
dehr <u>brah</u> • tuhn
roast

die Bratwurst
dee <u>braht</u> • voorst
fried sausage

die Ente
dee <u>ehn</u> • tuh
duck

das Filet
dahs <u>fee</u> • leh
filet

der Fleischkäse
dehr <u>fliesh</u> • kay • zuh
a kind of meatloaf

die Frikadelle
dee free • kah • <u>dehl</u> • luh
fried meatballs

das Gulasch
dahs <u>gool</u> • ahsh
stewed beef with spicy paprika gravy

der Hackbraten
dehr <u>hahk</u> • brah • tuhn
meatloaf

das Hackfleisch
dahs <u>hahk</u> • fliesh
ground meat

das Hühnchen
dahs <u>hewn</u> • khuhn
chicken

das Spanferkel
dahs <u>shpahn</u> • fehr • kehl
crunchy roasted suckling pig

das Kalbfleisch
dahs <u>kahlb</u> • fliesh
veal

das Kaninchen
dahs kah • <u>nihn</u> • khehn
rabbit

das Kotelett
dahs koht • <u>leht</u>
pork chop

das Lamm
dahs lahm
lamb

die Leber
dee <u>leh</u> • behr
liver

die Niere
dee <u>nee</u> • ruh
kidney

das Pökelfleisch
dahs <u>pehr</u> • kehl • fliesh
pickled meat

der Rinderbraten
dehr <u>reen</u> • dehr • brah • tuhn
roast beef

das Rindfleisch
dahs <u>rihnt</u> • fliesh
beef

die Rouladen
dee roo • <u>lah</u> • dehn
stuffed beef slices, rolled and braised in brown gravy

der Sauerbraten
dehr <u>zow</u> • ehr • brah • tuhn
beef roast, marinated with herbs, in a rich sauce

der Schinken ham
dehr <u>shihn</u> • kuhn

der Schinkenspeck bacon
dehr <u>shihn</u> • kuhn • shpehk

das Schmorfleisch stewed meat
dahs <u>shmohr</u> • fliesh

das Schweinefleisch pork
dahs <u>shvien</u> • uh • fliesh

der Schweinebraten roast pork
dehr <u>shvien</u> • brah • tuhn

das Steak steak
dahs shtayhk

der Tafelspitz Viennese-style boiled
dehr <u>tah</u> • fehl • shpeets beef

der Truthahn turkey
dehr <u>troot</u> • hahn

das Wiener Schnitzel veal cutlet
dahs <u>viee</u> • nehr <u>shniht</u> • tzehl

die Wurst sausage
dee voorst

die Zunge tongue
dee <u>tsoong</u> • uh

VEGETABLES & STAPLES

die Artischocke artichoke
dee ahr • tee • <u>shoh</u> • kuh

die Aubergine eggplant [aubergine]
dee <u>ow</u> • behr • gee • neh

die Avocado avocado
dee ah • voh • <u>kah</u> • doh

die Bohnen beans
dee <u>boh</u> • nuhn

die grünen Bohnen green beans
dee <u>grew</u> • nuhn boh • nuhn

der Blumenkohl	cauliflower
dehr <u>bloo</u> • muhn • kohl	
der Brokkoli	broccoli
dehr <u>broh</u> • koh • lee	
die Erbse	pea
dee <u>ehrb</u> • zuh	
das gemischte Gemüse	mixed vegetables
dahs geh • <u>meesh</u> • tuh geh • <u>mew</u> • zuh	
das Gemüse	vegetable
dahs geh • <u>mew</u> • zuh	
die Gurke	cucumber
dee <u>goor</u> • kuh	
die Kartoffel	potato
dee kahr • <u>toh</u> • fuhl	
der Kartoffelbrei	mashed potato
dehr kahr • <u>toh</u> • fehl • brie	
der Knoblauch	garlic
dehr <u>knoh</u> • blowkh	
der Kohl	cabbage
dehr kohl	
der Krautsalat	coleslaw
dehr <u>krowt</u> • sah • laht	
der Mais	corn
dehr mies	
der Maiskolben	corn on the cob
dehr <u>mies</u> • kohl • behn	
die Möhre	carrot
dee <u>mer</u> • ruh	
die Olive	olive
dee oh • <u>lee</u> • vuh	
der rote/grüne Paprika	red/green pepper
dehr <u>roh</u> • teh/ <u>grew</u> • neh pah • <u>pree</u> • kuh	
die Pasta	pasta
dee <u>pah</u> • stah	

die Pellkartoffeln
dee pehl • kahr • toh • fehl • ehn
boiled, unpeeled potatoes

der Pilz
dehr pihlts
mushroom

der Reis
dehr ries
rice

der Rettich
dehr reh • teekh
radish

das Roggenbrot
dahs roh • gehn • broht
rye bread

der Salat
dehr sah • laht
lettuce

der Spargel
dehr shpahr • gehl
asparagus

der Spinat
dehr shpee • naht
spinach

die Tomate
dee toh • mah • teh
tomato

die Zucchini
dee tsoo • khee • nee
zucchini [courgette]

die Zwiebel
dee tsvee • buhl
onion

FRUIT

die Ananas
dee ah • nah • nahs
pineapple

der Apfel
dehr ahp • fuhl
apple

die Apfelsine
dee ah • pfehl • zee • nuh
orange

die Banane
dee bah • nah • nuh
banana

die Birne
dee beer • nuh
pear

die Blaubeere	blueberry
dee blow • beh • ruh	
die Erdbeere	strawberry
dee ehrd • beh • ruh	
die Himbeere	raspberry
dee hihm • beh • ruh	
die Kirsche	cherry
dee keer • shuh	
die Limette	lime
dee lee • meh • tuh	
die Melone	melon
dee meh • loh • nuh	
das Obst	fruit
dahs ohpst	
die Pampelmuse	grapefruit
dee pahm • pehl • moo • zuh	
der Pfirsich	peach
dehr pfeer • zeekh	
die Pflaume	plum
dee pflow • muh	
die rote/schwarze Johannisbeere	red/black currant
dee roh • tuh/	
shvahr • tsuh yoh • hah • nihs • beh • ruh	

die Weintraube
dee <u>vien</u> • trow • buh

grape

die Zitrone
<u>dee tsee • troh</u> • nuh

lemon

CHEESE

der Appenzeller
dehr <u>ah</u> • pehn • tseh • lehr

hard cheese from Switzerland

der Blauschimmelkäse
dehr <u>blow</u> • shihm • mehl • kay • zuh

blue cheese

der Emmentaler
dehr <u>ehm</u> • mehn • tah • lehr

mild Swiss cheese

der Frischkäse
dehr <u>freesh</u> • kay • zuh

cream cheese

der Handkäse
dehr <u>hahnt</u> • kay • zuh

sharp, soft cheese

die Käseplatte
*dee <u>kay</u> • zuh • plah • tuh*r

cheese platte

der Schafskäse
dehr <u>shahf</u> • kay • zuh

feta cheese

der Tilsiter
dehr <u>teel</u> • seet • ehr

semi-soft Austrian cheese

der Ziegenkäse
dehr <u>tsee</u> • guhn • kay • zuh

goat cheese

DESSERT

der Apfelkuchen
dehr <u>ah</u> • pfuhl • kookh • uhn

apple pie or tart

das Eis
dahs ies

ice cream

der Käsekuchen
dehr <u>kay</u> • zuh • kookh • uhn

cheesecake

der Krapfen — fritter
dehr krah • pfehn

die Makrone — macaroon
dee mah • kroh • nuh

das Marzipan — marzipan
dahs mahr • tsee • pahn

der Obstsalat — fruit salad
dehr ohpst • sah • laht

die Rote Grütze — berry pudding
dee roh • tuh grewt • zuh

die Schwarzwälder Kirschtorte — Black Forest chocolate cake with cherries
dee schvahrts • vahl • dehr keersh • tohr • tuh

die Torte — cake
dee tohr • tuh

SAUCES & CONDIMENTS

salt — **salz**
sahlts

pepper — **pfeffer**
pfehf • fehr

mustard — **senf**
sehnf

ketchup — **ketchup**
ket • shahp

AT THE MARKET

Where are the trolleys/baskets? — **Wo sind die Einkaufswagen/ Einkaufskörbe?**
voh zihnt dee ien • kowfs • vah • guhn/ ien • kowfs • kehr • buh

Where is…?	**Wo ist …?**
	voh ihsht …
I'd like some of that/this.	**Ich möchte etwas von dem/diesem.**
	eekh merkh • tuh eht • vahs fohn dehm/dee • zuhm
Can I taste it?	**Kann ich es kosten?**
	kahn eekh ehs kohs • tuhn
I'd like…	**Ich möchte …**
	eekh merkh • tuh …
a kilo/	**ein Kilo/halbes Kilo …**
	ien kee • loh/
half-kilo of…	*hahl • buhs kee • loh …*
a liter of…	**einen Liter …**
	ien • uhn lee • tehr …
a piece of…	**ein Stück …**
	ien shtewk …
a slice of…	**eine Scheibe …**
	ien • uh shie • buh …
More/less	**Mehr/Weniger**
	mehr/veh • nee • guhr
How much?	**Wie viel kostet das?**
	vee feel kohs • tuht dahs
Where do I pay?	**Wo bezahle ich?**
	voh beht • sahl • uh eekh

A bag, please.

Eine Tüte, bitte.
ien • uh tew • tuh biht • tuh

I'm being helped.

Ich werde schon bedient.
eekh vehr • duh shohn buh • deent

YOU MAY HEAR...

Kann ich Ihnen helfen?
kahn eekh eehn • uhn hehl • fuhn

Can I help you?

Was möchten Sie?
vahs merkh • tuhn zee

What would you like?

Noch etwas?
nohkh eht • vahs

Anything else?

Das macht ... Euro.
dahs mahkht ... oy • roh

That's...euros.

Local markets that sell fresh produce and homemade goods can be found in most cities throughout Germany. The days and hours of operation vary widely. Your hotel concierge or a tourist information office can provide details.

For Meals & Cooking, see page 175.

IN THE KITCHEN

bottle opener

der Flaschenöffner
dehr flah • shuhn • erf • nehr

bowl

die Schüssel
dee shew • suhl

can opener

der Dosenöffner
dehr doh • zuhn • erf • nuhr

corkscrew	**der Korkenzieher**
	dehr kohr • kuhn • tsee • uhr
cup	**die Tasse**
	dee tah • suh
fork	**die Gabel**
	dee gah • buhl
frying pan	**die Bratpfanne**
	dee braht • pfah • nuh
glass	**das Glas**
	dahs glahs
(steak) knife	**das (Steak-) Messer**
	dahs (shtehk •) meh • sehr
measuring cup	**der Messbecher**
	dehr mehs • beh • khuhr
measuring spoon	**der Messlöffel**
	dehr mehs • ler • fuhl
napkin	**die Serviette**
	dee sehr • vyeh • tuh
plate	**der Teller**
	dehr teh • lehr
pot	**der Topf**
	dehr tohpf
spatula	**der Spatel**
	dehr shpah • tuhl
spoon	**der Löffel**
	dehr ler • fuhl

Measurements in Europe are metric – and that applies to the weight of food too. If you tend to think in pounds and ounces, it's worth brushing up on what the metric equivalent is before you go shopping for fruit and veg in markets and supermarkets. Five hundred grams, or half a kilo, is a common quantity to order, and that converts to just over a pound (17.65 ounces, to be precise).

DRINKS

NEED TO KNOW

The wine list/drink menu, please.	**Die Weinkarte/Getränkekarte, bitte.** *dee vien • kahr • tuh/* *geh • trehnk • uh • kahr • tuh biht • tuh*
What do you recommend?	**Was empfehlen Sie?** *vahs ehm • pfeh • luhn zee*
I'd like a bottle/glass of red/white wine.	**Ich möchte gern eine Flasche/ein Glas Rotwein/Weißwein.** *eekh merkh • tuh gehrn ien • uh* *flah • shuh/ien glahs roht • vien/* *vies • vien*
The house wine, please.	**Den Hauswein, bitte.** *dehn hows • vien biht • tuh*
Another bottle/glass, please.	**Noch eine Flasche/ein Glas, bitte.** *nohkh ien • uh flah • shuh/ien glahs* *biht • tuh*
I'd like a local beer.	**Ich möchte gern ein Bier aus der Region.** *eekh merkh • tuh* *gehrn ien beer ows dehr rehg • yohn*

Can I buy you a drink?	**Darf ich Ihnen einen ausgeben?**
	dahrf eekh <u>eehn</u> • uhn <u>ows</u> • geh • buhn
Cheers!	**Prost!**
	prohst
A coffee/tea, please.	**Einen Kaffee/Tee, bitte.**
	ien • uhn kah • <u>feh</u>/tee <u>biht</u> • tuh
Black.	**Schwarz.**
	shvahrts
With...	**Mit ...**
	miht ...
milk	**Milch**
	mihlkh
sugar	**Zucker**
	<u>tsoo</u> • kehr
artificial sweetener	**Süßstoff**
	<u>zews</u> • shtohf
..., please.	**..., bitte.**
	... <u>biht</u> • tuh
A juice	**Einen Saft**
	<u>ien</u> • uhn zahft
A soda	**Eine Cola**
	<u>ien</u> • uh <u>koh</u> • lah
A still/sparkling water	**Ein stilles Wasser/Wasser mit Kohlensäure**
	ien <u>shtihl</u> • uhs <u>vah</u> • sehr/<u>vah</u> • sehr miht <u>kohl</u> • ehn • zoy • ruh

NON-ALCOHOLIC DRINKS

die Cola
dee <u>koh</u> • lah   soda

Kaffee (coffee) is popular in Germany and a fresh cup can be found at a **Café** or **Kaffeehaus**. Kräutertee (herbal tea) is another common beverage, and pharmacies, supermarkets and health-food stores carry a variety of teas.

der Kaffee
dehr kah • feh coffee
der Kakao
dehr kah • kah • ow hot chocolate
die Milch
dee mihlkh milk
der Saft
dehr zahft juice
der (Eis-)Tee
dehr (ies) tee (iced) tea
das stille Wasser/Wasser mit Kohlensäure still/sparkling water
dahs shtihl • uh vah • sehr/vah • sehr miht kohl • ehn • zoy • ruh

YOU MAY HEAR...

Möchten Sie etwas trinken? Can I get you
merkh • tuhn zee eht • vahs trihn • kuhn a drink?
Mit Milch oder Zucker? With milk or
miht mihelkh oh • dehr tsoo • kehr sugar?
Stilles Wasser oder mit Kohlensäure? Still or sparkling
shtihl • uhs vah • sehr oh • dehr miht water?
koh • lehn • zoy • ruh

APERITIFS, COCKTAILS & LIQUEURS

der Gin — gin
dehr djihn

der Rum — rum
dehr room

der Scotch — scotch
dehr skohch

der Tequila — tequila
dehr teh • kee • lah

der Weinbrand — brandy
dehr vien • brahnt

der Whisky — whisky
dehr vees • kee

der Wodka — vodka
dehr voht • kah

BEER

as Flaschenbier — bottled beer
dahs flah • shuhn • beer

das Bier vom Fass — draft beer
dahs beer fohm fahs

There are more than 1,000 breweries in Germany, producing more than 5,000 different brands of beer. Styles include: **Altbier** (high hops content, similar to British ale), **Bockbier** (high malt content), **Hefeweizen** (pale, made from wheat), **Kölsch** (lager, brewed in Cologne), **Malzbier** (dark and sweet) and **Pilsener** (pale and strong). Popular German brands include: **Augustiner™**, **Beck's™**, **Jever™**, **Löwenbräu™** and **Spaten™**.

das Helle/Pilsner	lager/pilsner
dahs heh • luh/pihls • nehr	
die Halbe	pint
dee hahlb • uh	
das ... Bier	...beer
dahs ... beer	
dunkle/helle	dark/light
doon • kluh/heh • luh	
regionale/importierte	local/imported
reh • gyoh • nah • luh/ eem • pohr • teer • tuh	
alkoholfreie	non-alcoholic
ahl • koh • hohl • frie • uh	

WINE

der Champagner	champagne
dehr shahm • pahn • yehr	
der Wein	wine
dehr vien	
der Dessertwein	dessert wine
dehr deh • sehrt • vien	
der Hauswein/Tischwein	house/table wine

dehr <u>hows</u> • vien/<u>tihsh</u> • vien
der Rotwein/Weißwein — red/white wine
dehr <u>roht</u> • vien/<u>vies</u> • vien
der trockene/liebliche Wein — dry/sweet wine
dehr <u>troh</u> • keh • neh/<u>lee</u> • blee • kheh vien
der Schaumwein — sparkling wine
dehr <u>showm</u> • vien

ON THE MENU

der Aal *dehr ahl*	eel
die Ananas *dee <u>ahn</u> • ah • nahs*	pineapple
der Aperitif *dehr ah • pehr • ee • <u>teef</u>*	aperitif
der Apfel *dehr <u>ahp</u> • fehl*	apple
die Apfelsine *dee ah • pfuhl • <u>zee</u> • nuh*	orange
der Apfelwein *dehr <u>ah</u> • pfuhl • vien*	cider (alcoholic)
die Aprikose *dee ah • pree • <u>koh</u> • zuh*	apricot
die Artischocke *dee ahr • tee • <u>shoh</u> • kuh*	artichoke
die Aubergine *dee <u>ow</u> • behr • gee • nuh*	eggplant [aubergine]
der Aufschnitt *dehr <u>owf</u> • shniht*	cold cuts [charcuterie]
die Auster *dee <u>ows</u> • tuhr*	oyster
die Avocado *dee ah • voh • <u>kah</u> • doh*	avocado

die Backpflaume	prune
dee <u>bahk</u> • pflow • muh	
der Bacon	bacon
dehr <u>bah</u> • kohn	
die Banane	banana
dee bah • <u>nah</u> • nuh	
der Barsch	bass
dehr bahrsh	
das Basilikum	basil
dahs bah • <u>zee</u> • lee • koom	
das Bier	beer
dahs beer	
die Birne	pear
dee <u>beer</u> • nuh	
die Blaubeere	blueberry
dee <u>blow</u> • beh • ruh	
der Blauschimmelkäse	blue cheese
dehr <u>blow</u> • shihm • mel • kay • zuh	
der Blumenkohl	cauliflower
dehr <u>bloo</u> • muhn • kohl	
die Blutwurst	blood sausage
dee <u>bloot</u> • voorst	
die Bohne	bean
dee <u>boh</u> • nuh	

die Bouillon — broth
dee boo • yohn

der Branntwein — brandy
dehr brahnt • vien

der Braten — roast
dehr brah • tuhn

die Brombeere — blackberry
dee brohm • beh • ruh

das Brot — bread
dahs broht

das Brötchen — roll
dahs brert • khehn

die Brunnenkresse — watercress
dee broo • nuhn • kreh • zuh

die (Hühnchen-) Brust — breast (of chicken)
dee (hewn • khehn-) broost

die Butter — butter
dee boo • tehr

die Buttermilch — buttermilk
dee boo • tehr • mihlkh

die Cashewnuss — cashew
dee keh • shoo • noos

der Chikorée — chicory
dehr chee • koh • reh

die Chilischote — chili pepper
dee chee • lee • shoh • tuh

die Cola — soda
dee koh • lah

der Cracker — cracker
dehr kreh • kehr

die Datteln — dates
dee dah • tuhln

der Dessertwein — dessert wine
dehr deh • zehrt • vien

der Dill — dill
dehr dihl

der Donut — doughnut
dehr doh • nuht

der Dorsch — cod
dehr dohrsh

das Ei — egg
dahs ie

das Eigelb — egg yolk
dahs ie • gehlb

der Eierkuchen — pancake
dehr ier • koo • khuhn

das Eis — ice cream
dahs ies

der Eiswürfel — ice (cube)
dehr ies • vewr • fehl

das Eiweiß — egg white
dahs ie • vies

die Endivie — endive
dee ehn • dee • vee • uh

die Ente — duck
dee ehn • tuh

die Erbsen — peas
dee ehrb • zuhn

die Erdbeere — strawberry
dee ehrd • beh • ruh

die Erdnuss — peanut
dee ehrd • noos

der Essig — vinegar
dehr eh • zeek

das Estragon — tarragon
dahs eh • strah • gohn

der Fasan — pheasant
dehr fah • zahn

die Feige	fig
dee fie • guh	
der Fenchel	fennel
dehr fehn • khehl	
der Fisch	fish
dehr fihsh	
das Fleisch	meat
dahs fliesh	
die Fleischstücke	chopped meat
dee fliesh • shtew • kuh	
die Forelle	trout
dee foh • reh • luh	
die Gans	goose
dee gahns	
die Gänseleberpastete	goose liver pâté
dee gehn • zehl • leh • behr • pah • steh • tuh	
die Garnele	shrimp
dee gahr • neh • luh	
das Gebäck	pastry
dahs guh • behk	
das Geflügel	poultry
dahs guh • flew • gehl	
das Gemüse	vegetable
dahs geh • mew • zuh	

die Gewürze *dee guh • <u>vewr</u> • tsuh*	spices
die Gewürzgurke *dee guh • <u>vewrts</u> • goor • kuh*	pickle/gherkin
der Gin *dehr djihn*	gin
der Granatapfel *dehr grah • <u>naht</u> • ahp • fehl*	pomegranate
die grünen Bohnen *dee <u>grew</u> • nuhn <u>boh</u> • nuhn*	green beans
die Guave *dee <u>gwah</u> • veh*	guava
die Gurke *dee <u>goor</u> • kuh*	cucumber
die Hachse *dee <u>hahk</u> • suh*	shank
der Hamburger *dehr <u>hahm</u> • boor • gehr*	hamburger
der Hammel *dehr <u>hah</u> • mehl*	mutton
die Haselnuss *dee <u>hah</u> • zuhl • noos*	hazelnut
der Heilbutt *dehr <u>hiel</u> • boot*	halibut
die Henne *dee <u>heh</u> • nuh*	hen
der Hering *dehr <u>heh</u> • reeng*	herring
das Herz *dahs hehrts*	heart
die Himbeere *dee <u>heem</u> • beh • ruh*	raspberry
der Honig *dehr <u>hoh</u> • neek*	honey

der Hotdog	hot dog
dehr hoht • dohg	
das Hühnchen	chicken
dahs hewn • khehn	
der Hummer	lobster
dehr hoo • mehr	
der Hüttenkäse	cottage cheese
dehr hew • tuhn • kay • zuh	
der Imbiss	snack
dehr ihm • buhs	
der Ingwer	ginger
dehr eeng • vehr	
die Innereien	organ meat [offal]
dee ihn • eh • rie • uhn	
der Joghurt	yogurt
dehr yoh • goort	
der Kaffee	coffee
dehr kah • feh	
das Kalb	veal
dahs kahlb	
das Kaninchen	rabbit
dahs kah • neen • khehn	
die Kaper	caper
dee kah • pehr	
das Karamell	caramel
dahs kah • rah • mehl	
die Kartoffel	potato
dee kahr • toh • fehl	
die Kartoffelchips	potato chips [crisps]
dee kahr • toh • fehl • cheeps	
der Käse	cheese
dehr kay • zuh	
die Kastanie	chestnut
dee kah • stahn • yuh	

der Keks
dehr keks
cookie [biscuit]

der Kerbel
dehr kehr • behl
chervil

der Ketchup
dehr keh • chuhp
ketchup

die Kichererbse
dee kee • khehr • ehrb • zuh
chickpea

die Kirsche
dee keer • shuh
cherry

die Kiwi
dee kee • vee
kiwi

der Kloß
dehr klohs
dumpling

der Knoblauch
dehr knoh • blowkh
garlic

die Koblauchsauce
dee knoh • blowkh • zow • suh
garlic sauce

der Kohl
dehr kohl
cabbage

die Kokosnuss
dee koh • kohs • noos
coconut

das Kompott
dahs kohm • poht
stewed fruit

die Konfitüre
dee kohn • fee • tew • ruh
jelly

der Koriander
dehr koh • ree • ahn • dehr
cilantro [coriander]

die Kräuter
dee kroyt • uhr
herbs

die Kraftbrühe
dee krahft • brew • uh
consommé

der Krebs
dehr krehbs
crab

das Krustentier   shellfish
dahs kroos•tehn•tyehr

der Kuchen   pie
dehr kookh•uhn

der Kümmel   caraway
dehr kew•mehl

der Kürbis   squash
dehr kewr•bees

die Kutteln   tripe
dee koo•tehln

der Lachs   salmon
dehr lahks

das Lamm   lamb
dahs lahm

die Lauchzwiebel   scallion [spring onion]
dee lowkh•svee•buhl

die Leber   liver
dee leh•buhr

die Lende   loin
dee lehn•duh

das Lendenfilet   sirloin
dahs lehn•dehn•fee•leh

der Likör   liqueur
dehr lee•ker

die Limette   lime
dee lee•meh•tuh

die Limonade   lemonade
dee lee•moh•nah•duh

die Linse   lentil
dee leen•zuh

das Loorbeerblatt   bay leaf
dahs lohr•behr•blaht

der Mais   sweet corn
dehr mies

das Maismehl
dahs <u>mies</u> • mehl

cornmeal

die Makkaroni
dee mah • kah • <u>roh</u> • nee

macaroni

die Makrele
dee mah • <u>krehl</u> • uh

mackerel

die Mandarine
dee mahn • dah • <u>reen</u> • uh

tangerine

die Mandel
dee <u>mahn</u> • duhl

almond

die Mango
dee <u>mahn</u> • goh

mango

die Margarine
dee mahr • guh • <u>ree</u> • nuh

margarine

die Marmelade
dee mahr • muh • <u>lah</u> • duh

marmalade/jam

das Marzipan
dahs <u>mahr</u> • tsee • pahn

marzipan

die Mayonnaise
dee mah • yoh • <u>nay</u> • zuh

mayonnaise

die Meerbarbe
dee <u>mehr</u> • bahr • buh

red mullet

die Meeresfrüchte
dee <u>meh</u> • rehs • frewkh • tuh

seafood

die Melone
dee meh • loh • nuh
melon

die Milch
dee mihlkh
milk

das Milchmixgetränk
dahs mihlkh • mihks • geh • traynk
milk shake

die Minze
dee mihn • tsuh
mint

die Möhre
dee mer • ruh
carrot

die Muschel
dee moo • shehl
clam

der Muskat
dehr moos • kaht
nutmeg

die Nelke
dee nehl • kuh
clove

die Niere
dee nee • ruh
kidney

die Nudel
dee noo • dehl
noodle

der Nugat
dehr noo • gaht
nougat

die Nüsse
dee new • suh
nuts

das Obst
dahs ohbst
fruit

der Ochse
dehr ohkh • suh
ox

der Ochsenschwanz
dehr ohk • sehn • shvahnts
oxtail

der Oktopus
dehr ohk • toh • poos
octopus

die Olive
dee oh • lee • veh
olive

das Olivenöl
dahs oh • lee • vehn • erl

olive oil

das Omelett
dahs ohm • leht

omelet

der Orangenlikör
dehr oh • rahn • jehn • lee • ker

orange liqueur

das Oregano
dahs oh • reh • gah • noh

oregano

die Pampelmuse
dee pahm • puhl • moo • zuh

grapefruit

der Pansen
dehr pahn • sehn

tripe

die Papaya
dee pah • pah • yah

papaya

der Paprika
dehr pah • pree • kuh

paprika

die Paprikaschote
dee pah • pree • kah • shoh • tuh

pepper (vegetable)

die Pastinake
dee pah • stee • nahk • uh

parsnip

die Pekannuss
dee peh • kahn • noos

pecan

das Perlhuhn
dahs pehrl • hoon

guinea fowl

die Petersilie
dee peh • tehr • see • lee • uh

parsley

der Pfannkuchen
dehr pfahn • koo • khuhn

pancake

der Pfeffer
dehr pfeh • fehr

pepper (seasoning)

der Pfirsich
dehr pfeer • zeekh

peach

die Pflaume
dee pflow • muh

plum

der Pilz	mushroom
dehr pihlts	
die Pizza	pizza
dee pee • tsah	
die Pommes frites	French fries
dee pohm freets	
der Porree	leek
dehr poh • reh	
der Portwein	port
dehr pohrt • vien	
die Preiselbeere	cranberry
dee prie • zuhl • beh • ruh	
der Rahmkäse	cream cheese
dehr rahm • kay • zuh	
der Reis	rice
dehr ries	
der Rettich	radish
dehr reh • teekh	
der Rhabarber	rhubarb
dehr rah • bahr • behr	
der Rinderbraten	roast beef
dehr reen • dehr • brah • tuhn	
das Rindfleisch	beef
dahs rihnt • fliesh	

der Rosenkohl — Brussels sprouts
dehr roh • zuhn • kohl

die Rosine — raisin
dee roh • zee • nuh

der Rosmarin — rosemary
dehr rohs • mah • reen

die rote Johannisbeere — red currant
dee roh • tuh yoh • hah • nihs • beh • ruh

der Rotkohl — red cabbage
dehr roht • kohl

die Rübe — beet/turnip
dee rew • beh

der Rum — rum
dehr room

der Safran — saffron
dehr zahf • rahn

der Saft — juice
dehr zahft

die Sahne — cream
dee zah • nuh

die Salami — salami
dee zah • lah • mee

der Salat — lettuce/salad
dehr sah • laht

der Salbei — sage
dehr zahl • bie

das Salz — salt
dahs zahlts

das Sandwich — sandwich
dahs sahnd • weetsh

die Sardelle — anchovy
dee sahr • dehl • uh

die Sardine — sardine
dee zahr • dee • nuh

die Sauce sauce
dee zows • uh

die Sauerkirsche sour cherry
dee zow • ehr • keer • shuh

die saure Sahne sour cream
dee zow • ruh zah • nuh

die Schalotte shallot
dee shah • loh • tuh

die scharfe Pfeffersauce hot pepper sauce
dee shahr • fuh pfeh • fehr • zow • suh

das Schaumgebäck meringue
dahs showm • guh • behk

der Schellfisch haddock
dehr shehl • fihsh

der Schinken ham
dehr sheen • kuhn

die Schlagsahne whipped cream
dee shlahg • zah • nuh

die Schnecke snail
dee shnehkh • uh

der Schnittlauch chives
dehr shniht • lowkh

das Schnitzel chop
dahs shniht • tzuhl

die Schokolade chocolate
dee shoh • koh • lah • duh

die Schulter shoulder
dee shool • tehr

die schwarze Johannisbeere black currant
dee shvahr • tsuh yoh • hah • nees • beh • ruh

das Schweinefleisch pork
dahs shvien • uh • fliesh

der Schwertfisch swordfish
dehr shvehrt • fihsh

der Scotch	scotch
dehr skohtsh	
der Seebarsch	sea bass
dehr <u>zeh</u> • bahrsh	
der Seehecht	hake
dehr <u>zeh</u> • hehkht	
der Seeteufel	monkfish
dehr <u>zeh</u> • toy • fuhl	
die Seezunge	sole
dee <u>zeh</u> • tsoong • uh	
der Sellerie	celery
dehr <u>zeh</u> • luh • ree	
der Senf	mustard
dehr zehnf	
der Sherry	sherry
dehr <u>shehr</u> • ee	
der Sirup	syrup
dehr <u>zew</u> • roop	
das Soda-Wasser	soda water
dahs <u>soh</u> • dah-<u>vah</u> • sehr	
die Sojabohne	soybean [soya bean]
dee <u>zoh</u> • yah • boh • nuh	
die Sojamilch	soymilk [soya milk]
dee <u>zoh</u> • yah • mihlkh	

die Sojasauce
dee zoh • yah • zow • suh

soy sauce

die Sojasprossen
dee soh • jah • shproh • suhn

bean sprouts

die Spaghetti
dee shpah • geh • tee

spaghetti

das Spanferkel
dahs shpahn • fehr • kehl

crunchy roasted
suckling pig

der Spargel
dehr shpahr • gehl

asparagus

der Spinat
dehr shpee • naht

spinach

die Spirituosen
dee shpee • ree • twoh • zuhn

spirits

die Stachelbeere
dee shtah • khehl • beh • ruh

gooseberry

das Steak
dahs stehk

steak

die Suppe
dee zoo • puh

soup

die Süßigkeiten
dee zew • seekh • kie • tuhn

candy [sweets]

die Süßkartoffel
dee zews • kahr • toh • fuhl

sweet potato

die süßsaure Sauce — sweet and sour sauce
dee zews • zow • ruh zow • suh

der Süßstoff — sweetener
dehr zews • shtohf

der Tee — tea
dehr teh

der Thunfisch — tuna
dehr toon • fihsh

der Thymian — thyme
dehr tew • mee • ahn

der Tintenfisch — squid
dehr teen • tuhn • fihsh

der Toast — toast
dehr tohst

das Tofu — tofu
dahs toh • foo

die Tomate — tomato
dee toh • mah • tuh

das Tonic — tonic water
dahs toh • neek

die Trüffel — truffles
dee trew • fuhl

der Truthahn — turkey
dehr troot • hahn

die Vanille — vanilla
dee vah • nee • luh

die Wachtel — quail
dee vahkh • tehl

die Waffel — waffle
dee vah • fuhl

die Walnuss — walnut
dee vahl • noos

das Wasser — water
dahs vah • sehr

die Wassermelone	watermelon
dee <u>vah</u> • sehr • meh • loh • nuh	
der Wein	wine
dehr vien	
die Weintrauben	grapes
dee <u>vien</u> • trow • buhn	
der Weizen	wheat
dehr <u>vie</u> • tsuhn	
der Wermut	vermouth
dehr <u>vehr</u> • moot	
der Whisky	whisky
dehr <u>vees</u> • kee	
das Wild	game/venison
dahs vihlt	
der Wodka	vodka
dehr <u>vohd</u> • kah	
die Wurst	sausage
dee voorst	
der Zackenbarsch	sea perch
dehr <u>tsah</u> • kehn • bahrsh	
das Zicklein	kid (young goat)
dahs <u>tsihk</u> • lien	
die Ziege	goat
dee <u>tsee</u> • guh	

der Ziegenkäse
dehr <u>tsee</u> • guhn • kay • zuh

goat cheese

der Zimt
dehr tsihmt

cinnamon

die Zitrone
dee tsee • <u>troh</u> • nuh

lemon

die Zucchini
dee tsoo • <u>kee</u> • nee

zucchini [courgette]

der Zucker
dehr <u>tsoo</u> • kehr

sugar

die Zunge
dee <u>tsoong</u> • uh

tongue

die Zwiebel
dee <u>tsvee</u> • buhl

onion

PEOPLE

GOING OUT

NEED TO KNOW

What's there to do at night?	**Was kann man dort abends unternehmen?** *vahs kahn mahn dohrt ahb • uhnds oon • tehr • nehm • uhn*
Do you have a program of events?	**Haben Sie ein Veranstaltungsprogramm?** *hah • buhn zee ien fehr • ahn • shtahlt • oongs • prohg • rahm*
What's playing tonight?	**Was wird heute Abend aufgeführt?** *vahs vihrd hoyt • uh ahb • uhnd owf • guh • fewrt*
Where's...?	**Wo ist ...?** *voh ihst ...*
the downtown area	**das Stadtzentrum** *dahs shtadt • tsehn • troom*
the bar	**die Bar** *dee bahr*

the dance club	**der Tanzclub**
	dee tahnts • kloop
Is there a cover charge?	**Kostet es Eintritt?**
	kohs • tuht ehs ien • triht

ENTERTAINMENT

Can you recommend…?	**Können Sie … empfehlen?**
	kern • uhn zee … ehm • pfeh • luhn
a concert	**ein Konzert**
	ien kohn • tsehrt
a movie	**einen Film**
	ien • uhn feelm
an opera	**eine Oper**
	ien • uhn oh • pehr
a play	**ein Theaterstück**
	ien teh • ah • tehr • shtewk
When does it start/end?	**Wann beginnt/endet es?**
	vahn beh • gihnt/ehnd • eht ehs
Where's…?	**Wo ist …?**
	voh ihst …
the concert hall	**die Konzerthalle**
	dee kohn • tsehrt • hah • luh
the opera house	**das Opernhaus**
	dahs oh • pehrn • hows
the theater	**das Theater**
	dahs teh • ah • tehr
the arcade	**die Spielhalle?**
	dee shpeel • hah • luh
What's the dress code?	**Wie ist die Kleiderordnung?**
	vee ihst dee klied • ehr • ohrd • noong
I like…	**Mir gefällt …**
	meer guh • fehlt …

ⓘ

Bitte schalten Sie Ihre Handys aus.
biht • tuh shahlt • uhn zee eehr • uh hehnd • ees ows

Turn off your mobile [cell] phones, please.

classical music	**klassische Musik**
	klahs • ihsh • uh moo • zeek
folk music	**Volksmusik**
	fohlks • moo • zeek
jazz	**Jazz**
	djehz
pop music	**Popmusik**
	pohp • moo • zeek
rap	**Rap**
	rehp

For Tickets, see page 47.

NIGHTLIFE

What's there to do at night?	**Was kann man dort abends unternehmen?**
	vahs kahn mahn dohrt ahb • uhnds oont • ehr • nehm • uhn
Can you recommend…?	**Können Sie … empfehlen?**
	kern • uhn zee … ehm • pfeh • luhn
a bar	**eine Bar**
	ien • uh bahr
a cabaret	**eine Kabarettvorstellung**
	ie • nuh kah • bah • reht • fohr • shteh • loong
a casino	**ein Casino**
	ien kah • see • noh

a dance club	**einen Tanzclub** *ien • uhn <u>tahnts</u> • kloop*
a gay club	**einen Schwulenclub** *ien • uhn <u>shvoo</u> • luhn • kloop*
a jazz club	**einen Jazzclub** *ien • uhn <u>yahts</u> • kloop*
a club with German music	**ein Club mit deutscher Musik** *ien cloob meet doyt • <u>shuhr</u> muh • seek*
Is there live music?	**Gibt es dort Livemusik?** *gihpt ehs dohrt liev • moo • <u>zeek</u>*
How do I get there?	**Wie komme ich dorthin?** *vee <u>kohm</u> • uh eekh dohrt • <u>hihn</u>*
Is there a cover charge?	**Kostet es Eintritt?** *<u>kohs</u> • tuht ehs <u>ien</u> • triht*
Let's go dancing.	**Lass uns tanzen gehen.** *ahs oons <u>tahnt</u> • suhn <u>geh</u> • uhn*
Is this area safe at night?	**Ist dieses Gebiet bei Nacht sicher?** *ihst dee • zuhs geh • beet bie nahkht <u>zeek</u> • hehr*

ROMANCE

NEED TO KNOW

Would you like to go out for a drink/dinner?	**Möchten Sie mit mir auf einen Drink/zum Essen gehen?** _merkh_ • _tuhn zee miht meer owf_ _ien_ • _uhn treenk/tsoom eh_ • _suhn_ _geh_ • _uhn_
What are your plans for tonight/tomorrow?	**Was haben Sie heute Abend/morgen vor?** _vahs hah_ • _buhn zee hoy_ • _tuh_ _ah_ • _buhnt/mohr_ • _guhn fohr_
Can I have your number?	**Kann ich Ihre Telefonnummer haben?** _kahn eekh ee_ • _ruh_ _teh_ • _leh_ • _fohn_ • _noo_ • _mehr hah_ • _buhn_
Can I join you?	**Kann ich mitkommen?** _kahn eekh miht_ • _koh_ • _muhn_
Can I get you a drink?	**Darf ich Ihnen einen Drink ausgeben?** _dahrf eekh eehn_ • _uhn ien_ • _uhn treenk_ _ows_ • _geh_ • _buhn_
I like/love you.	**Ich mag/liebe dich.** _eekh mahk/lee_ • _buh deekh_

THE DATING GAME

Would you like to go out... for coffee?	**Möchten Sie mit mir Kaffee trinken gehen?** _mehrkh_ • _tuhn zee miht meer ien_ • _uhn_ _kah_ • _feh trihnk_ • _uhn geh_ • _uhn_

Would you like to go out for a drink?	**Möchten Sie mit mir etwas trinken gehen?**
	merkht • uhn zee eht • vahs thrihn • khun geh • huhn
Would you like to go out for dinner?	**Möchten Sie mit mir etwas essen gehen?**
	merkht • uhn zee eht • vahs ehs • suhn geh • huhn
What are your plans for... ?	**Was haben Sie ... vor?**
	vahs <u>hah</u> • buhn zee ... fohr
today	**heute**
	<u>hoy</u> • tuh
tonight	**heute Abend**
	<u>hoy</u> • tuh <u>ah</u> • buhnt
tomorrow	**morgen**
	mohr • guhn
this weekend	**dieses Wochenende**
	dee • zuhs voh • <u>khuhn</u> • <u>ehn</u> • duh
Where would you like to go?	**Wohin möchten Sie gern gehen?**
	<u>voh</u> • hihn <u>merkh</u> • tuhn zee gehrn <u>geh</u> • uhn
I'd like to go...	**Ich möchte gern ... gehen.**
	eekh <u>merkh</u> • tuh gehrn ...<u>geh</u> • uhn
Do you like...?	**Mögen Sie ...?**
	<u>mer</u> • guhn zee ...
Can I have your number/e-mail?	**Kann ich Ihre Telefonnummer/E-Mail haben?**
	kahn eekh <u>ee</u> • ruh teh • leh • <u>fohn</u> • noo • mehr/<u>ee</u> • mehl <u>hah</u> • buhn
Are you on Facebook/Twitter?	**Sind Sie bei Facebook/Twitter?**
	(polite form)
	zihnt zee by face • book/twit • ter
Can I join you?	**Kann ich mitkommen?**
	kahn eekh <u>miht</u> • koh • muhn

You're very attractive. **Sie sind sehr attraktiv.**
zee zihnt zehr aht • rahk • teef

Let's go somewhere quieter. **Lassen Sie uns an einen ruhigeren Ort gehen.**
lah • suhn zee oons ahn ien • uhn roo • ee • geh • ruhn ohrt geh • uhn

For Communications, see page 86.

ACCEPTING & REJECTING

I'd love to. **Gerne.**
gehr • nuh

Where should we meet? **Wo wollen wir uns treffen?**
voh voh • luhn veer oons treh • fuhn

I'll meet you at the bar/your hotel. **Ich treffe Sie an der Bar/Ihrem Hotel.**
eekh treh • fuh zee ahn dehr bahr/ ee • ruhm hoh • tehl

I'll come by at… **Ich komme um … vorbei.**
eekh koh • muh oom … fohr • bie

What is your address? **Wie ist Ihre Adresse?**
vee ihsht ee • ruh ah • drehs • uh

I'm busy. **Ich bin beschäftigt.**
eekh been beh • shehf • teekt

I'm not interested. **Ich habe kein Interesse.**
eekh hah • buh kien in • teh • reh • suh

Leave me alone. **Lassen Sie mich in Ruhe.**
lah • sehn zee meekh ihn roo • uh

Stop bothering me! **Hören Sie auf, mich zu belästigen!**
her • ruhn zee owf meekh tsoo buh • lay • steeg • uhn

For Time, see page 25.

GETTING INTIMATE

Can I hug/kiss you?	**Kann ich dich umarmen/küssen?**
	kahn eekh deekh <u>oom</u>•ahr•muhn/
	<u>kew</u>•zuhn
Yes.	**Ja.**
	yah
No.	**Nein.**
	nien
Stop!	**Stopp!**
	shtohp
I like/love you.	**Ich mag/liebe dich.**
	eekh mahk/<u>lee</u>•buh deekh

SEXUAL PREFERENCES

Are you gay?	**Bist du schwul?**
	beesht doo shvool
I'm…	**Ich bin …**
	eekh been …
heterosexual	**heterosexuell**
	heh•tuh•roh•<u>sehks</u>•oo•ehl
homosexual	**homosexuell**
	hoh•moh•<u>sehks</u>•oo•ehl
bisexual	**bisexuell**
	bee•<u>sehks</u>•oo•ehl
Do you like men/ women?	**Magst du Männer/Frauen?**
	mahgst doo <u>meh</u>•nehr/<u>frow</u>•uhn

Altmarkt

DICTIONARY

ENGLISH–GERMAN

A

accept *v* akzeptieren
access *n* der Zutritt
accident der Unfall
accommodation die Unterkunft
account *n* **(bank)** das Konto
acupuncture die Akupunktur
adapter der Adapter
address *n* die Adresse
admission (price) der Eintritt
after nach; **~noon** der Nachmittag; **~shave** das Aftershave
age *n* das Alter
agency die Agentur
AIDS AIDS
air *n* die Luft; **~ conditioning** die Klimaanlage; **~-dry** lufttrocknen; **~ pump** die Luftpumpe; **~line** die Fluggesellschaft; **~mail** die Luftpost; **~plane** das Flugzeug; **~port** der Flughafen
aisle der Gang; **~ seat** der Platz am Gang

allergic allergisch; **~ reaction** die allergische Reaktion
allow erlauben
alone allein
alter *v* umändern
alternate route die Alternativroute
aluminum foil die Aluminiumfolie
amazing erstaunlich
ambulance der Krankenwagen
American *adj* amerikanisch
amusement park der Vergnügungspark
anemic anämisch
anesthesia die Anästhesie
animal das Tier
ankle das Fußgelenk
antibiotic *n* das Antibiotikum
antiques store das Antiquitätengeschäft
antiseptic cream die antiseptische Creme
apartment das Apartment
appendix (body part) der Blinddarm

adj adjective	**BE** British English	**prep** prepostion
adv adverb	**n** noun	**v** verb

appetizer die Vorspeise

appointment der Termin

arcade die Spielhalle

area code die Ortsvorwahl

arm n (body part) der Arm

aromatherapy die
Aromatherapie

around (the corner) um;
~ (price) ungefähr

arrival Ankunft

arrive ankommen

artery die Arterie

arthritis die Arthritis

art die Kunst

Asian adj asiatisch

aspirin das Aspirin

asthmatic asthmatisch

ATM der Bankautomat;
~ card die Bankkarte

attack v angreifen

attraction (place)
die Sehenswürdigkeit

attractive attraktiv

Australia das Australien

Australian adj australisch

automatic automatisch;
~ car das Auto mit
Automatikschaltung

available verfügbar

B

baby das Baby;
~ bottle die Babyflasche;
~ wipe das Baby-Pflegetuch;
~sitter der Babysitter

back (body part) der Rücken;
~ache die
Rückenschmerzen;
~pack der Rucksack

bag die Tasche

baggage [BE] das Gepäck;
~ claim die Gepäckausgabe;
~ ticket der Gepäckschein

bake v backen

bakery die Bäckerei

ballet das Ballett

bandage das Pflaster

bank n die Bank

bar (place) die Bar

barbecue (device) n der Grill

barber der Herrenfriseur

baseball der Baseball

basket (grocery store)
der Einkaufskorb

basketball der Basketball

bathroom das Bad

battery die Batterie

battleground das
Schlachtfeld

be v sein

beach der Strand

beautiful wunderschön; ~
schön

bed n das Bett; ~ and
breakfast
die Pension

before vor

begin beginnen

beginner der Anfänger

behind (direction) hinter

beige *adj* beige
belt der Gürtel
best *adj* beste; ~ **before** mindestens haltbar bis
better besser
bicycle das Fahrrad
big groß; ~**ger** größerger
bike route die Radroute
bikini der Bikini
bill *n* (**money**) der Geldschein; ~ *n* (**of sale**) die Rechnung
bird der Vogel
birthday der Geburtstag
black *adj* schwarz
bladder die Blase
bland fad
blanket die Decke
bleed bluten
blender der Mixer
blood das Blut; ~ **pressure** der Blutdruck
blouse die Bluse
blue *adj* blau
board *v* einsteigen; ~**ing pass** die Bordkarte
boat *n* das Boot
boil *v* kochen
bone *n* der Knochen
book *n* das Buch; ~**store** der Buchladen
boot *n* der Stiefel
boring langweilig
botanical garden der botanische Garten
bother *v* belästigen

bottle *n* die Flasche; ~ **opener** der Flaschenöffner
bowl *n* die Schüssel
boxing match der Boxkampf
boy der Junge; ~**friend** der Freund
bra der BH
bracelet das Armband
brake (car) die Bremse
breaded paniert
break *v* (**bone**) brechen
breakdown (car) die Panne
breakfast *n* das Frühstück
break-in (burglary) *n* der Einbruch
breast die Brust; ~**feed** *v* stillen
breathe atmen
bridge die Brücke
briefs (clothing) der Schlüpfer
bring bringen
British *adj* britisch
broken kaputt; ~ (**bone**) gebrochen
brooch die Brosche
broom der Besen
brother der Bruder
brown *adj* braun
bug (insect) *n* das Insekt
building das Gebäude
burn *v* brennen
bus *n* der Bus; ~ **station** der Busbahnhof; ~ **stop** die Bushaltestelle;

~ **ticket** die Busfahrkarte;
~ **tour** die Busreise
business *adj* Geschäfts-;
~ **card** die Visitenkarte;
~ **center** das
Geschäftszentrum;
~ **class** die Business-Class;
~ **hours** die Öffnungszeiten
butcher *n* der Fleischer
buttocks der Po
buy *v* kaufen
bye auf Wiedersehen

C

cabaret das Kabarett
cable car die Seilbahn
cafe (place) das Café
call *v* **(phone)** anrufen;
~ *n* der Anruf ~ **collect** ein
R-Gespräch führen
calorie die Kalorie
camera die Kamera;
~ **case** die Kameratasche;
digital ~ die Digitalkamera
camp *v* campen; ~**ing stove**
der Campingkocher;
~**site** der Campingplatz
can opener der Dosenöffner
Canada das Kanada
Canadian *adj* kanadisch
cancel stornieren
candy die Süßigkeit
canned good die Konserve
canyon der Canyon
car das Auto;

~ **hire [BE]** die
Autovermietung; ~ **park [BE]**
der Parkplatz;
~ **rental** die Autovermietung;
~ **seat** der Autositz
carafe die Karaffe
card *n* die Karte;
ATM ~ die Bankkarte;
credit ~ die Kreditkarte;
debit ~ die EC-Karte;
phone ~ die Telefonkarte
carry-on *n* **(piece of hand
luggage)** das
Handgepäckstück
cart (grocery store) der
Einkaufswagen; ~ **(luggage)**
der Gepäckwagen
carton (of cigarettes) die
Stange (Zigaretten);
~ **(of groceries)** die Packung
cash *n* das Bargeld;
~ *v* einlösen
cashier der Kassierer
casino das Casino
castle das Schloss
cathedral die Kathedrale
cave *n* die Höhle
CD die CD
cell phone das Handy
Celsius Celsius
centimeter der Zentimeter
certificate das Zertifikat
chair *n* der Stuhl;
~ **lift** der Sessellift
change *v* **(baby)** wickeln;

~ **(buses)** umsteigen;
~ **(money)** wechseln;
~ n **(money)** das Wechselgeld
charge v **(credit card)** belasten; ~ **(cost)** verlangen
cheap billig; **~er** billiger
check v **(luggage)** aufgeben; ~ **(on something)** prüfen; n **(payment)** der Scheck; **~-in** das Check-in; **~ing account** das Girokonto; **~-out** das Check-out
Cheers! Prost!
chemical toilet die Campingtoilette
chemist [BE] die Apotheke
chest (body part) die Brust; ~ **pain** die Brustschmerzen
chewing gum der Kaugummi
child das Kind; **~'s seat** der Kinderstuhl
children's menu das Kindermenü
children's portion die Kinderportion
Chinese adj chinesisch
chopsticks die Stäbchen
church die Kirche
cigar die Zigarre
cigarette die Zigarette
class n die Klasse; **business** ~ die Business-Class; **economy** ~ die Economy-Class; **first** ~ die erste Klasse
classical music die klassische Musik
clean v reinigen; ~ adj **(clothes)** sauber; **~ing product** das Reinigungsmittel
clear v **(on an ATM)** löschen
cliff die Klippe
cling film [BE] die Klarsichtfolie
close v **(a shop)** schließen
closed geschlossen
clothing die Bekleidung; ~ **store** das Bekleidungsgeschäft
club n der Club
coat der Mantel
coin die Münze
colander das Sieb
cold n **(sickness)** die Erkältung; ~ adj **(temperature)** kalt
colleague der Kollege
cologne das Kölnischwasser
color n die Farbe
comb n der Kamm
come v kommen
complaint die Beschwerde
computer der Computer
concert das Konzert; ~ **hall** die Konzerthalle
condition (medical) die Beschwerden
conditioner (hair) die

Spülung
condom das Kondom
conference die Konferenz
confirm bestätigen
congestion (medical) der Blutstau
connect (internet) verbinden
connection (travel/internet) die Verbindung; ~ **flight** der Anschlussflug
constipated verstopft
consulate das Konsulat
consultant der Berater
contact v kontaktieren
contact lens die Kontaktlinse;
~ **solution** Kontaktlinsenlösung
contagious ansteckend
convention hall der Kongresssaal
conveyor belt das Förderband
cook v kochen
cool adj **(temperature)** kalt
copper n das Kupfer
corkscrew n der Korkenzieher
cost v kosten
cotton die Baumwolle
cough v husten;
~ n der Husten
country code die Landesvorwahl
cover charge der Preis pro Gedeck

cream (ointment) die Creme
credit card die Kreditkarte
crew neck der runde Halsausschnitt
crib das Kinderbett
crystal n **(glass)** das Kristall
cup n die Tasse
currency die Währung;
~ **exchange** der Währungsumtausch;
~ **exchange office** die Wechselstube
current account [BE] das Girokonto
customs der Zoll
cut v schneiden;
~ n **(injury)** der Schnitt
cute süß
cycling das Radfahren

D

damage v beschädigen
dance v tanzen; ~ **club** der Tanzclub; ~**ing** das Tanzen
dangerous gefährlich
dark adj dunkel
date n **(calendar)** das Datum
day der Tag
deaf adj taub
debit card die EC-Karte
deck chair der Liegestuhl
declare v **(customs)** deklarieren
decline v **(credit card)** ablehnen

deep *adj* tief
degree (temperature) das Grad
delay *v* verzögern
delete *v* **(computer)** löschen
delicatessen das Feinkostgeschäft
delicious lecker
denim das Denim
dentist der Zahnarzt
denture die Zahnprothese
deodorant das Deodorant
department store das Kaufhaus
departure (plane) der Abflug
deposit *v* **(money)** einzahlen; ~ *n* **(bank)** die Einzahlung
desert *n* die Wüste
detergent das Waschmittel
develop *v* **(film)** entwickeln
diabetic *adj* diabetisch; *n* der Diabetiker
dial *v* wählen
diamond der Diamant
diaper die Windel
diarrhea der Durchfall
diesel der Diesel
difficult schwierig
digital digital; ~ **camera** die Digitalkamera; ~ **photo** das Digitalfoto; ~ **print** der digitale Ausdruck
dining room das Esszimmer
dinner das Abendessen
direction die Richtung

dirty schmutzig
disabled *adj* **(person)** behindert; ~ **accessible [BE]** behindertengerecht
disconnect (computer) trennen
discount *n* der Rabatt; die Ermäßigung
dishes (kitchen) das Geschirr
dishwasher der Geschirrspüler
dishwashing liquid das Geschirrspülmittel
display *n* **(device)** das Display; ~ **case** die Vitrine
disposable *n* der Einwegartikel; ~ **razor** der Einweg-Rasierer
dive *v* tauchen
diving equipment die Tauchausrüstung
divorce *v* sich scheiden lassen
dizzy *adj* schwindelig
doctor *n* der Arzt
doll *n* die Puppe
dollar (U.S.) der Dollar
domestic inländisch; ~ **flight** der Inlandsflug
door die Tür
dormitory der Schlafsaal
double bed das Doppelbett
downtown *n* das Stadtzentrum
dozen das Dutzend

drag lift der Schlepplift
dress (clothing) das Kleid;
   ~ **code** die Kleiderordnung
drink v trinken; ~ n das
   Getränk; ~ **menu** die
   Getränkekarte; **~ing water**
   das Trinkwasser
drive v fahren
driver's license number die
   Führerscheinnummer
drop n **(medicine)** der Tropfen
drowsiness die Schläfrigkeit
dry clean chemisch reinigen;
   ~er's die chemische
   Reinigung
dubbed synchronisiert
during während
duty (tax) der Zoll; **~-free**
   zollfrei
DVD die DVD

E

ear das Ohr; **~ache** die
   Ohrenschmerzen
earlier früher
early früh
earring der Ohrring
east n der Osten
easy leicht
eat v essen
economy class die Economy-
   Class
elbow n der Ellenbogen
electric outlet die Steckdose
elevator der Fahrstuhl

e-mail v eine E-Mail senden;
   ~ n die E-Mail; ~ **address** die
   E-Mail-Adresse
emergency der Notfall;
   ~ **exit** der Notausgang
empty v entleeren
end v beenden; ~ n das Ende
engaged (person) verlobt
English adj englisch; ~ n
   (language) das Englisch
engrave eingravieren
enjoy genießen
enter v **(place)** eintreten
entertainment die
   Unterhaltung
entrance der Eingang
envelope der Umschlag
epileptic adj epileptisch;
   ~n der Epileptiker
equipment die Ausrüstung
escalator die Rolltreppe
e-ticket das E-Ticket
EU resident der EU-Bürger
euro der Euro
evening n der Abend
excess baggage das
   Übergepäck
exchange v umtauschen;
   ~ n **(place)** die
   Wechselstube; ~ **rate** der
   Wechselkurs
excursion der Ausflug
excuse v entschuldigen
exhausted erschöpft
exit v verlassen; ~ n der

Ausgang
expensive teuer
experienced erfahren
expert der Experte
exposure (film) die
Belichtung
express *adj* Express-; ~ **bus**
der Expressbus; ~ **train** der
Expresszug
extension (phone) die
Durchwahl
extra *adj* zusätzlich; ~ **large**
extragroß
extract *v* **(tooth)** ziehen
eye das Auge
eyebrow wax
die Augenbrauenkorrektur

F

face *n* das Gesicht
facial *n* die kosmetische
Gesichtsbehandlung
family *n* die Familie
fan *n* **(appliance)** der
Ventilator
far (distance) weit
farm der Bauernhof
far-sighted weitsichtig
fast *adj* schnell
fat free fettfrei
father der Vater
fax *v* faxen; ~ *n* das Fax;
~ **number** die Faxnummer
fee *n* die Gebühr
feed *v* füttern

ferry *n* die Fähre
fever *n* das Fieber
field (sports) der Platz
fill *v* **(car)** tanken
fill out *v* **(form)** ausfüllen
filling *n* **(tooth)** die Füllung
film *n* **(camera)** der Film
fine *n* **(fee for breaking law)**
die Strafe
finger *n* der Finger; ~**nail** der
Fingernagel
fire *n* das Feuer;
~ **department** die
Feuerwehr; ~ **door** die
Feuertür
first *adj* erste; ~ **class** erste
Klasse
fit *n* **(clothing)** die Passform
fitting room die
Umkleidekabine
fix *v* **(repair)** reparieren
fixed-price menu
das Festpreismenü
flash photography das
Fotografieren mit Blitzlicht
flashlight das Blitzlicht
flight *n* der Flug
flip-flops die Badelatschen
floor *n* **(level)** die Etage
florist der Florist
flower *n* die Blume
folk music die Volksmusik
food das Essen; ~ **processor**
die Küchenmaschine
foot *n* der Fuß

football game [BE] das Fußballspiel

for für

forecast *n* die Vorhersage

forest *n* der Wald

fork *n* die Gabel

form *n* **(document)** das Formular

formula (baby) die Babynahrung

fort die Festung

fountain *n* der Springbrunnen

free *adj* frei

freelance work die freiberufliche Arbeit

freezer der Gefrierschrank

fresh frisch

friend der Freund

frozen food die Tiefkühlkost

frying pan die Bratpfanne

full-time *adj* Vollzeit-

G

game *n* das Spiel

garage *n* **(parking)** die Garage; ~ *n* **(for repairs)** die Autowerkstatt

garbage bag der Abfallbeutel

gas (car) das Benzin; ~ **station** die Tankstelle

gate (airport) das Gate

gay *adj* **(homosexual)** schwul; ~ **bar** die Schwulenbar; ~ **club** der Schwulenclub

gel *n* **(hair)** das Gel

generic drug das Generikum

German *adj* deutsch; ~ *n* **(language)** das Deutsch

Germany Deutschland

get off (a train/bus/ subway) aussteigen

gift *n* das Geschenk; ~ **shop** der Geschenkwarenladen

girl das Mädchen; ~**friend** die Freundin

give *v* geben

glass (drinking) das Glas; ~ **(material)** das Glas

glasses die Brille

go *v* **(somewhere)** gehen

gold *n* das Gold

golf *n* das Golf; ~ **course** der Golfplatz; ~ **tournament** das Golfturnier

good *adj* gut; ~ *n* die Ware; ~ **afternoon** guten Tag ~ **day** guten Tag; ~ **evening** guten Abend; ~ **morning** guten Morgen; ~**bye** auf Wiedersehen

gram das Gramm

grandchild das Enkelkind

grandparents die Großeltern

gray *adj* grau

green *adj* grün

grocery store das Lebensmittelgeschäft

ground floor das Erdgeschoss

groundcloth die Unterlegplane

group n die Gruppe
guide n **(book)** der Reiseführer; ~ n **(person)** der Fremdenführer ~ **dog** der Blindenhund
gym n **(place)** der Fitnessraum
gynecologist der Gynäkologe

H

hair das Haar; ~**brush** die Haarbürste; ~**cut** der Haarschnitt; ~ **dryer** der Fön; ~ **salon** der Friseursalon; ~**spray** das Haarspray; ~**style** die Frisur; ~ **stylist** der Friseur
halal halal
half adj halb; ~ n die Hälfte; ~ **hour** die halbe Stunde; ~-**kilo** das halbe Kilo
hammer n der Hammer
hand n die Hand; ~ **luggage** das Handgepäck; ~ **wash** die Handwäsche; ~**bag [BE]** die Handtasche
handicapped behindert; ~-**accessible** behindertengerecht
hangover der Kater
happy glücklich
hat der Hut
have v haben; ~ **sex** Sex haben

hay fever der Heuschnupfen
head (body part) n der Kopf; ~**ache** die Kopfschmerzen; ~**phones** die Kopfhörer
health die Gesundheit; ~ **food store** das Reformhaus
hearing impaired hörgeschädigt
heart das Herz; ~ **condition** die Herzkrankheit
heat v heizen; ~**er** das Heizgerät; ~**ing [BE]** die Heizung
hectare der Hektar
hello Hallo
helmet der Helm
help v helfen; ~ n die Hilfe
here hier
hi Hallo
high hoch; ~**chair** der Kindersitz; ~**lights (hair)** die Strähnchen; ~**way** die Autobahn
hiking boots die Wanderschuhe
hill n der Berg
hire v **[BE] (a car)** mieten; ~ **car [BE]** das Mietauto
hockey das Hockey
holiday [BE] der Urlaub
horsetrack die Pferderennbahn
hospital das Krankenhaus
hostel die Jugendherberge
hot (spicy) scharf;

~ **(temperature)** heiß;
~ **spring** heiße Quelle;
~ **water** heißes Wasser
hotel das Hotel
hour die Stunde
house n das Haus; **~hold
goods** die Haushaltswaren;
~keeping services der
Hotelservice
how wie; ~ **much** wie viel
hug v umarmen
hungry hungrig
hurt v wehtun
husband der Ehemann

I

ibuprofen das Ibuprofen
ice n das Eis; ~ **hockey** das
Eishockey
icy eisig
identification die
Identifikation
ill krank
in in
include v beinhalten
indoor pool (public) das
Hallenbad
inexpensive preisgünstig
infected infiziert
information (phone) die
Auskunft; ~ **desk** die
Information
insect das Insekt: ~ **bite** der
Insektenstich; ~ **repellent**
der Insektenschutz

insert v **(card)** einführen
insomnia die Schlaflosigkeit
instant message die instant
Message
insulin das Insulin
insurance die Versicherung;
~ **card** die
Versicherungskarte;
~ **company** die
Versicherungsgesellschaft
interesting interessant
intermediate fortgeschritten
international international;
~ **flight** der internationale
Flug; ~ **student card**
der internationale
Studentenausweis
internet das Internet;
~ **cafe** das Internetcafé;
~ **service** der Internetservice
interpreter der Dolmetscher
intersection die Kreuzung
intestine der Darm
introduce v
(person) vorstellen
invoice n **[BE]** die Rechnung
Ireland das Irland
Irish adj irisch
iron v bügeln; ~ n
(clothes) das Bügeleisen
Italian adj italienisch

J

jacket n die Jacke
Japanese adj japanisch

jar n (for jam etc.) das Glas
jaw n der Kiefer
jazz n der Jazz; ~ **club** der Jazzclub
jeans die Jeans
jet ski n die Jet-Ski
jeweler der Juwelier
jewelry der Schmuck
join v (go with somebody) mitkommen
joint n (body part) das Gelenk

K

key n der Schlüssel; ~ **card** die Schlüsselkarte; ~**ring** der Schlüsselring
kiddie pool das Kinderbecken
kidney (body part) die Niere
kilo das Kilo; ~**gram** das Kilogramm; ~**meter** der Kilometer
kiss v küssen
kitchen die Küche; ~ **foil** [BE] die Aluminiumfolie
knee n das Knie
knife das Messer
kosher adj koscher

L

lace n (fabric) die Spitze
lactose intolerant laktoseintolerant
lake der See
large groß

last adj letzte
late (time) spät
launderette [BE] der Waschsalon
laundromat der Waschsalon
laundry (place) die Wäscherei ~ **service** der Wäscheservice
lawyer n der Anwalt
leather n das Leder
leave v (hotel) abreisen; ~ (plane) abfliegen
left adj, adv (direction) links
leg n das Bein
lens die Linse
less weniger
lesson n die Lektion; **take ~s** Unterricht nehmen
letter n der Brief
library die Bücherei
life jacket die Schwimmweste
lifeguard der Rettungsschwimmer
lift n [BE] der Fahrstuhl; ~ n (ride) die Mitfahrgelegenheit; ~ **pass** der Liftpass
light n (cigarette) das Feuer; ~ n (overhead) die Lampe; ~**bulb** die Glühbirne
lighter n das Feuerzeug
like v mögen
line n (train/bus) die Linie
linen das Leinen
lip n die Lippe

liquor store das Spirituosengeschäft
liter der Liter
little wenig
live v leben; ~ **music** Livemusik
liver (body part) die Leber
loafers die Halbschuhe
local n **(person)** der Einheimische
lock v abschließen; ~ n das Schloss
locker das Schließfach
log off v **(computer)** abmelden
log on v **(computer)** anmelden
long adj lang; ~**-sighted [BE]** weitsichtig; ~**-sleeved** langärmlig
look v schauen; ~ **for something** etwas suchen
loose (fit) locker
lose v **(something)** verlieren
lost verloren; ~**-and-found** das Fundbüro
lotion die Lotion
louder lauter
love v **(someone)** lieben; ~ n die Liebe
low adj niedrig
luggage das Gepäck; ~ **cart** der Gepäckwagen; ~ **locker** das Gepäckschließfach; ~ **ticket** der Gepäckschein

lunch n das Mittagessen
lung die Lunge
luxury car das Luxusauto

M

machine washable maschinenwaschbar
magazine das Magazin
magnificent großartig
mail v mit der Post schicken; ~ n die Post; ~**box** der Briefkasten
main attraction die Hauptattraktion
main course das Hauptgericht
mall das Einkaufszentrum
man (adult male) der Mann
manager der Manager
manicure n die Maniküre
manual car das Auto mit Gangschaltung
map n die Karte; ~ n **(town)** der Stadtplan
market n der Markt
married verheiratet
marry heiraten
mass n **(church service)** die Messe
massage n die Massage
match n das Spiel
meal die Mahlzeit
measure v **(someone)** Maß nehmen
measuring cup der

Messbecher
measuring spoon der Messlöffel
mechanic n der Mechaniker
medication (drugs) die Medikamente
medicine das Medikament
medium (steak) medium
meet v treffen
meeting n **(business)** das Meeting; **~ room** das Konferenzzimmer
membership card der Mitgliedsausweis
memorial (place) das Denkmal
memory card die Speicherkarte
mend v **(clothes)** ausbessern
menstrual cramps die Menstruationskrämpfe
menu (restaurant) die Speisekarte
message die Nachricht
meter n **(parking)** die Parkuhr; **~** n **(measure)** der Meter
microwave n die Mikrowelle
midday [BE] der Mittag
midnight die Mitternacht
mileage die Meilenzahl
mini-bar die Mini-Bar
minute die Minute
missing (not there) weg
mistake n der Fehler

mobile home der Wohnwagen
mobile phone [BE] das Handy
mobility die Mobilität
monastery das Kloster
money das Geld
month der Monat
mop n der Wischmopp
moped das Moped
more mehr
morning n der Morgen
mosque die Moschee
mother n die Mutter
motion sickness die Reisekrankheit
motor n der Motor; **~ boat** das Motorboot; **~cycle** das Motorrad; **~way [BE]** die Autobahn
mountain der Berg; **~ bike** das Mountainbike
mousse (hair) der Schaumfestiger
mouth n der Mund
movie der Film; **~ theater** das Kino
mug v überfallen
multiple-trip ticket der Mehrfachfahrschein
muscle n der Muskel
museum das Museum
music die Musik; **~ store** das Musikgeschäft

N

nail file die Nagelfeile
nail salon das Nagelstudio
name *n* der Name
napkin die Serviette
nappy [BE] die Windel
nationality die Nationalität
nature preserve das Naturreservat
nausea die Übelkeit
nauseous übel
near nahe; **~-sighted** kurzsichtig
nearby in der Nähe von
neck *n* der Nacken
necklace die Kette
need *v* brauchen
newspaper die Zeitung
newsstand der Zeitungskiosk
next *adj* nächste
nice schön
night die Nacht; **~club** der Nachtclub
no nein; **~ (not any)** kein
non-alcoholic nichtalkoholisch
non-smoking *adj* Nichtraucher
noon *n* der Mittag
north *n* der Norden
nose die Nase
note *n* **[BE] (money)** der Geldschein
nothing nichts

notify *v* benachrichtigen
novice der Anfänger
now jetzt
number *n* die Nummer
nurse *n* die Krankenschwester

O

office das Büro; **~ hours** die Bürozeiten
off-licence [BE] das Spirituosengeschäft
oil *n* das Öl
OK okay
old *adj* alt
on the corner an der Ecke
once (one time) einmal
one ein; **(counting)** eins; **~-day (ticket)** Tages-; **~-way ticket (airline)** das einfache Ticket, **(bus/train/subway)** die Einzelfahrkarte; **~-way street** die Einbahnstraße
only nur
open *v* öffnen; **~** *adj* offen
opera die Oper; **~ house** das Opernhaus
opposite *n* das Gegenteil
optician der Optiker
orange *adj* **(color)** orange
orchestra das Orchester
order *v* **(restaurant)** bestellen
outdoor pool das Freibad
outside *prep* draußen

over *prep* **(direction)** über;
~**done (meat)** zu lang
gebraten; ~**heat** *v* **(car)**
überhitzen; ~**look** *n*
(scenic place) der
Aussichtsplatz; ~**night**
über Nacht; ~**-the-counter**
(medication) rezeptfrei
oxygen treatment
die Sauerstoffbehandlung

P

p.m. nachmittags
pacifier der Schnuller
pack *v* packen
package *n* das Paket
pad *n* [BE] die Monatsbinde
paddling pool [BE]
das Kinderbecken
pain der Schmerz
pajamas der Pyjama
palace der Palast
pants die Hose
pantyhose die Strumpfhose
paper *n* **(material)** das
Papier; ~ **towel** das
Papierhandtuch
paracetamol [BE] das
Paracetamol
park *v* parken; ~ *n* der Park;
~**ing garage** das Parkhaus;
~**ing lot** der Parkplatz;
~**ing meter** die Parkuhr
parliament building
das Parlamentsgebäude

part (for car) das Teil;
~**-time** *adj* Teilzeit-
pass through *v* **(travel)**
durchreisen
passenger der Passagier
passport der Reisepass;
~ **control** die Passkontrolle
password das Passwort
pastry shop die Konditorei
patch *v* **(clothing)** ausbessern
path der Pfad
pay *v* bezahlen; ~**phone**
das öffentliche Telefon
peak *n* der Gipfel
pearl *n* die Perle
pedestrian *n* der Fußgänger
pediatrician der Kinderarzt
pedicure *n* die Pediküre
pen *n* der Stift
penicillin das Penicillin
penis der Penis
per pro; ~ **day** pro Tag;
~ **hour** pro Stunde;
~ **night** pro Nacht;
~ **week** pro Woche
perfume *n* das Parfüm
period (menstrual) die
Periode; ~ **(of time)** der
Zeitraum
permit *v* erlauben
petrol [BE] das Benzin;
~ **station** [BE] die Tankstelle
pewter das Zinn
pharmacy die Apotheke
phone *v* anrufen; ~ *n* das

Telefon; ~ **call** das Telefonat;
~ **card** die Telefonkarte;
~ **number** die
Telefonnummer
photo das Foto; ~**copy** die
Fotokopie;
~**graphy** die Fotografie
pick up v **(person)** abholen
picnic area der Rastplatz
piece n das Stück
Pill (birth control) die Pille
pillow n das Kissen
pink adj rosa
piste [BE] die Piste; ~ **map**
[BE] der Pistenplan
pizzeria die Pizzeria
place v **(a bet)** abgeben
plane n das Flugzeug
plastic wrap die Klarsichtfolie
plate n der Teller
platform [BE] (train) der
Bahnsteig
platinum n das Platin
play v spielen; ~ n **(theatre)**
das Stück; ~**ground** der
Spielplatz; ~**pen** der
Laufstall
please adv bitte
pleasure n die Freude
plunger die Saugglocke
plus size die Übergröße
pocket n die Tasche
poison n das Gift
poles (skiing) die Stöcke
police die Polizei;

~ **report** der Polizeibericht;
~ **station** das Polizeirevier
pond n der Teich
pool n der Pool
pop music die Popmusik
portion n die Portion
post n **[BE]** die Post;
~ **office** die Post;
~**box [BE]** der Briefkasten;
~**card** die Postkarte
pot n der Topf
pottery die Töpferwaren
pound n **(weight)** das Pfund;
~ **(British sterling)** das
Pfund
pregnant schwanger
prescribe (medication)
verschreiben
prescription das Rezept
press v **(clothing)** bügeln
price n der Preis
print v drucken; ~ n der
Ausdruck
problem das Problem
produce n das Erzeugnis;
~ **store** das
Lebensmittelgeschäft
prohibit verbieten
pronounce aussprechen
Protestant der Protestant
public adj öffentlich
pull v ziehen
purple adj violett
purse n die Handtasche
push v drücken; ~**chair [BE]**

der Kinderwagen

Q

quality *n* die Qualität
question *n* die Frage
quiet *adj* leise

R

racetrack die Rennbahn
racket *n* **(sports)** der Schläger
railway station [BE] der Bahnhof
rain *n* der Regen; **~coat** die Regenjacke; **~forest** der Regenwald; **~y** regnerisch
rap *n* **(music)** der Rap
rape *v* vergewaltigen; **~** *n* die Vergewaltigung
rare selten
rash *n* der Ausschlag
ravine die Schlucht
razor blade die Rasierklinge
reach *v* erreichen
ready bereit
real *adj* echt
receipt *n* die Quittung
receive *v* erhalten
reception (hotel) die Rezeption
recharge *v* aufladen
recommend empfehlen
recommendation die Empfehlung
recycling das Recycling

red *adj* rot
refrigerator der Kühlschrank
region die Region
registered mail das Einschreiben
regular *n* **(fuel)** das Normalbenzin
relationship die Beziehung
rent *v* mieten; **~** *n* die Miete
rental car das Mietauto
repair *v* reparieren
repeat *v* wiederholen
reservation die Reservierung; **~ desk** der Reservierungsschalter
reserve *v* **(hotel)** reservieren
restaurant das Restaurant
restroom die Toilette
retired *adj* **(from work)** in Rente
return *v* **(something)** zurückgeben; **~** *n* **[BE] (trip)** die Hin- und Rückfahrt
reverse *v* **(the charges) [BE]** ein R-Gespräch führen
rib *n* **(body part)** die Rippe
right *adj, adv* **(direction)** rechts; **~ of way** die Vorfahrt
ring *n* der Ring
river der Fluss
road map die Straßenkarte
rob *v* berauben
robbed beraubt
romantic *adj* romantisch

room *n* das Zimmer; ~ **key** der Zimmerschlüssel; ~ **service** der Zimmerservice
round trip die Hin- und Rückfahrt
route *n* die Route
rowboat das Ruderboot
rubbing alcohol der Franzbranntwein
rubbish *n* [BE] der Abfall; ~ **bag** [BE] der Abfallbeutel
rugby das Rugby
ruin *n* die Ruine
rush *n* die Eile

S

sad traurig
safe *adj* (protected) sicher; ~ *n* (thing) der Safe
sales tax die Mehrwertsteuer
same *adj* gleiche
sandals die Sandalen
sanitary napkin die Monatsbinde
sauna die Sauna
sauté *v* sautieren
save *v* (computer) speichern
savings (account) das Sparkonto
scanner der Scanner
scarf der Schal
schedule *v* planen; ~ *n* der Plan
school *n* die Schule
science die Wissenschaft

scissors die Schere
sea das Meer
seat *n* der Sitzplatz
security die Sicherheit
see *v* sehen
self-service *n* die Selbstbedienung
sell *v* verkaufen
seminar das Seminar
send *v* senden
senior citizen der Rentner
separated (person) getrennt lebend
serious ernst
service (in a restaurant) die Bedienung
sexually transmitted disease (STD) die sexuell übertragbare Krankheit
shampoo *n* das Shampoo
sharp *adj* scharf
shaving cream die Rasiercreme
sheet *n* (bed) die Bettwäsche
ship *v* versenden
shirt das Hemd
shoe store das Schuhgeschäft
shoe der Schuh
shop *v* einkaufen; ~ *n* das Geschäft
shopping *n* das Einkaufen; ~ **area** das Einkaufszentrum; ~ **centre** [BE] das Einkaufszentrum;

~ **mall** das Einkaufszentrum
short kurz; ~-**sleeved**
kurzärmelig
shorts die kurze Hose
short-sighted [BE] kurzsichtig
shoulder n die Schulter
show v zeigen
shower n (bath) die Dusche
shrine der Schrein
sick adj krank
side n die Seite; ~ **dish**
die Beilage; ~ **effect** die
Nebenwirkung; ~ **order** die
Beilage
sightseeing das Besichtigen
von Sehenswürdigkeiten;
~ **tour** die Besichtigungstour
sign v
(document) unterschreiben
silk die Seide
silver n das Silber
single adj
(person) alleinstehend;
~ **bed** das Einzelbett;
~ **print** der Einzelabzug;
~ **room** das Einzelzimmer
sink n das Waschbecken
sister die Schwester
sit v sitzen
size n die Größe
ski v Ski fahren; ~ n der Ski;
~ **lift** der Skilift
skin n die Haut
skirt n der Rock
sleep v schlafen; ~**er car**

der Schlafwagen; ~**ing bag**
der Schlafsack; ~**ing car** [BE]
der Schlafwagen
slice n die Scheibe
slippers die Pantoffeln
slower langsamer
slowly langsam
small klein
smoke v rauchen
smoking (area) Raucher-
snack bar der Imbiss
sneakers die Turnschuhe
snowboard n das Snowboard
snowshoe n der
Schneeschuh
snowy verschneit
soap n die Seife
soccer der Fußball
sock die Socke
some (with singular nouns)
etwas; ~ (with plural nouns)
einige
soother [BE] der Schnuller
sore throat die
Halsschmerzen
south n der Süden
souvenir n das Souvenir;
~ **store** das Souvenirgeschäft
spa das Wellness-Center
spatula der Spatel
speak v sprechen
specialist (doctor) der
Spezialist
specimen die Probe
speeding die Geschwindig-

keitsüberschreitung
spell v buchstabieren
spicy scharf; **~ (not bland)** würzig
spine (body part) die Wirbelsäule
spoon n der Löffel
sports der Sport; **~ massage** die Sportmassage
sprain n die Verstauchung
stadium das Stadion
stairs die Treppe
stamp v **(ticket)** entwerten; **~** n **(postage)** die Briefmarke
start v beginnen
starter [BE] die Vorspeise
station n **(stop)** die Haltestelle; **bus ~** der Busbahnhof; **gas ~** die Tankstelle; **petrol ~ [BE]** die Tankstelle; **subway ~** die U-Bahn-Haltestelle; **train ~** der Bahnhof
statue die Statue
steakhouse das Steakhouse
steal v stehlen
steep adj steil
sterling silver das Sterlingsilber
sting n der Stich
stolen gestohlen
stomach der Magen; **~ache** die Bauchschmerzen

stool (bowel movement) der Stuhlgang
stop v **(bus)** anhalten; **~** n **(transportation)** die Haltestelle
store directory (mall) der Übersichtsplan
storey [BE] die Etage
stove n der Herd
straight adv **(direction)** geradeaus
strange seltsam
stream n der Strom
stroller (baby) der Kinderwagen
student (university) der Student; **~ (school)** der Schüler
study v studieren; **~ing** n das Studieren
stuffed gefüllt
stunning umwerfend
subtitle n der Untertitel
subway die U-Bahn; **~ station** die U-Bahn Haltestelle
suit n der Anzug; **~case** der Koffer
sun n die Sonne; **~block** das Sonnenschutzmittel; **~burn** der Sonnenbrand; **~glasses** die Sonnenbrille; **~ny** sonnig; **~screen** die Sonnencreme; **~stroke** der Sonnenstich
super n **(fuel)** das Superbenzin; **~market** der

Supermarkt
surfboard das Surfboard
surgical spirit [BE] der Franzbranntwein
swallow v schlucken
sweater der Pullover
sweatshirt das Sweatshirt
sweet n [BE] die Süßigkeit; ~ adj (taste) süß
swelling die Schwellung
swim v schwimmen; ~suit der Badeanzug
symbol (keyboard) das Zeichen
synagogue die Synagoge

T

table n der Tisch
tablet (medicine) die Tablette
take v nehmen
tampon n der Tampon
taste v (test) kosten
taxi n das Taxi
team n das Team
teaspoon der Teelöffel
telephone n das Telefon
temple (religious) der Tempel
temporary vorübergehend
tennis das Tennis
tent n das Zelt; ~ **peg** der Zelthering; ~ **pole** die Zeltstange
terminal n (airport) der Terminal
terrible schrecklich

text v (send a message) eine SMS schicken; ~ n der Text
thank v danken; ~ **you** vielen Dank
the der?, das (neuter), die/
theater das Theater
theft der Diebstahl
there dort
thief der Dieb
thigh der Oberschenkel
thirsty durstig
this dieser?, dieses (neuter), diese/
throat der Hals
thunderstorm das Gewitter
ticket n die Fahrkarte; ~ **office** der Fahrkartenschalter
tie n (clothing) die Krawatte
tight (fit) eng
tights [BE] die Strumpfhose
time die Zeit; ~**table [BE]** (transportation) der Fahrplan
tire n der Reifen
tired müde
tissue das Gewebe
tobacconist der Tabakhändler
today adv heute
toe n der Zeh
toenail der Zehnagel
toilet [BE] die Toilette; ~ **paper** das Toilettenpapier

tomorrow *adv* morgen
tongue *n* die Zunge
tonight heute Abend
to *(direction)* zu
tooth der Zahn
toothpaste die Zahnpasta
total *n (amount)* der Gesamtbetrag
tough *adj (food)* zäh
tour *n* die Tour
tourist der Tourist; ~ **information office** das Touristeninformationsbüro
tow truck der Abschleppwagen
towel *n* das Handtuch
tower *n* der Turm
town die Stadt; ~ **hall** das Rathaus; ~ **map** der Stadtplan; ~ **square** der Rathausplatz
toy das Spielzeug; ~ **store** der Spielzeugladen
track *n (train)* der Bahnsteig
traditional traditionell
traffic light die Ampel
trail *n (ski)* die Piste; ~ **map** der Pistenplan
trailer (car) der Anhänger
train *n* der Zug; ~ **station** der Bahnhof
transfer *v (change trains/ flights)* umsteigen; ~ **(money)** überweisen
translate übersetzen

trash *n* der Abfall
travel *n* das Reisen; ~ **agency** das Reisebüro; ~ **sickness** die Reisekrankheit; ~**ers check [cheque BE]** der Reisescheck
tree der Baum
trim (hair) *v* nachschneiden
trip *n* die Reise
trolley [BE] (grocery store) der Einkaufswagen; ~ **[BE] (luggage)** der Gepäckwagen
trousers [BE] die Hose
T-shirt das T-Shirt
tumble dry maschinentrocknen
turn off *v* **(device)** ausschalten
turn on *v* **(device)** anschalten
TV der Fernseher
tyre [BE] der Reifen

U

ugly hässlich
umbrella der Regenschirm
unbranded medication [BE] das Generikum
unconscious (faint) bewusstlos
underdone halb gar
underground *n* **[BE]** die U-Bahn; ~ **station [BE]** die U-Bahn-Haltestelle
underpants [BE] der Slip

understand *v* verstehen
underwear die Unterwäsche
United Kingdom (U.K.)
das Großbritannien
United States (U.S.)
die Vereinigten Staaten
university die Universität
unleaded (gas) bleifrei
upset stomach
die Magenverstimmung
urgent dringend
urine der Urin
use *v* benutzen
username der Benutzername
utensil das Haushaltsgerät

V

vacancy (room) das freie
Zimmer
vacation der Urlaub
vaccination die Impfung
vacuum cleaner der
Staubsauger
vaginal infection die vaginale
Entzündung
valid gültig
valley das Tal
valuable *adj* wertvoll
value *n* der Wert
van der Kleintransporter
VAT [BE] die Mehrwertsteuer
vegan *n* der Veganer;
~ *adj* vegan
vegetarian *n* der Vegetarier;
~ *adj* vegetarisch

vehicle registration
die Fahrzeugregistrierung
viewpoint (scenic) [BE]
der Aussichtsplatz
village das Dorf
vineyard das Weingut
visa das Visum
visit *v* besuchen; **~ing hours**
die Besuchszeiten
visually
impaired sehbehindert
vitamin das Vitamin
V-neck der V-Ausschnitt
volleyball game das
Volleyballspiel
vomit *v* erbrechen;
~ing das Erbrechen

W

wait *v* warten;
~ *n* die Wartezeit
waiter der Kellner
waiting room der Warteraum
waitress die Kellnerin
wake *v* wecken;
~-up call der Weckruf
walk *v* spazieren gehen;
~ *n* der Spaziergang;
~ing route die Wanderroute
wallet die Geldbörse
war memorial
das Kriegsdenkmal
warm *v*
(something) erwärmen;
~ *adj* **(temperature)** warm

washing machine die
  Waschmaschine
watch v beobachten
waterfall der Wasserfall
wax v (hair) mit Wachs
  entfernen (Haare)
weather n das Wetter
week die Woche; ~end das
  Wochenende
weekly wöchentlich
welcome adj willkommen;
  you're ~ gern geschehen
west n der Westen
what was
wheelchair der Rollstuhl;
  ~ ramp die Rollstuhlrampe
when adv (at what
  time) wann
where wo
white adj weiß; ~ gold das
  Weißgold
who (question) wer
widowed verwitwet
wife die Ehefrau
window das Fenster;
  ~ case das Schaufenster
wine list die Weinkarte

wireless wireless; ~ phone
  das schnurlose Telefon
with mit
withdraw v (money) abheben;
  ~al (bank) die Abhebung
without ohne
woman die Frau
wool die Wolle
work v arbeiten
wrap v einpacken
wrist das Handgelenk
write v schreiben

Y

year das Jahr
yellow adj gelb
yes ja
yesterday adv gestern
young adj jung
youth hostel
  die Jugendherberge

Z

zoo der Zoo

GERMAN–ENGLISH

A

der Abend evening
das Abendessen dinner
der Abfall *n* trash [rubbish BE]
der Abfallbeutel garbage [rubbish BE] bag
abfliegen *v* leave (plane)
der Abflug departure (plane)
abgeben *v* place (a bet)
abheben *v* withdraw (money)
die Abhebung withdrawal (bank)
abholen *v* pick up (something)
ablehnen *v* decline (credit card)
abmelden *v* log off (computer)
der Abschleppwagen tow truck
abschließen *v* lock (door)
der Adapter adapter
die Adresse *n* address
das Aftershave aftershave
die Agentur agency
AIDS AIDS
die Akupunktur *n* acupuncture
akzeptieren *v* accept
allein alone; **~stehend** single (person)
allergisch allergic;
die allergische

Reaktion allergic reaction
alt *adj* old
das Alter *n* age
die Alternativroute alternate route
die Aluminiumfolie aluminum [kitchen BE] foil
amerikanisch American
die Ampel traffic light
anämisch anemic
die Anästhesie anesthesia
der Anfänger beginner/novice
angreifen *v* attack
anhalten *v* stop
der Anhänger trailer
ankommen arrive
die Ankunft arrival
anmelden *v* log on (computer)
der Anruf *n* call
anrufen *v* call
anschalten *v* turn on (device)
ansteckend contagious
das Antibiotikum *n* antibiotic
das Antiquitätengeschäft antiques store
antiseptisch antiseptic
der Anwalt lawyer
die Anzahlung *n* deposit (car rental)
der Anzug *n* suit
das Apartment apartment

die **Apotheke** pharmacy
[chemist BE]
arbeiten v work
arbeitslos adj unemployed
der **Arm** n arm (body part)
die **Aromatherapie** aromatherapy
die **Arterie** artery
die **Arthritis** arthritis
der **Arzt** doctor
asiatisch Asian
das **Aspirin** aspirin
asthmatisch asthmatic
atmen breathe (place)
attraktiv attractive
auf Wiedersehen goodbye
aufladen v recharge
das **Auge** eye
ausbessern v mend (clothing)
der **Ausfluss** discharge (bodily
fluid)
ausfüllen v fill out (form)
der **Ausgang** n exit
ausgeschlafen well-rested
die **Auskunft** information
(phone)
die **Ausrüstung** equipment
ausschalten turn off (device)
der **Ausschlag** rash
der **Aussichtsplatz** viewpoint
[BE]
aussprechen pronounce
aussteigen get off (a train/
bus/subway)
Australien Australia

der **Australier** Australian
das **Auto** car; ~ **mit**
Automatikschaltung
automatic car; ~ **mit**
Gangschaltung manual car
die **Autobahn** highway
[motorway BE]
automatisch automatic
der **Autositz** car seat
die **Autovermietung** car
rental [hire BE]

B

das **Baby** baby
die **Babyflasche** baby bottle
die **Babynahrung** formula
(baby)
das **Baby-Pflegetuch** baby
wipe
der **Babysitter** babysitter
backen bake
die **Bäckerei** bakery
das **Bad** bathroom
der **Badeanzug** swimsuit
die **Badelatschen** flip-flops
der **Bahnhof** train [railway BE]
station
der **Bahnsteig** track [platform
BE]
das **Ballett** ballet
die **Bank** bank (money)
der **Bankautomat** ATM
die **Bankkarte** ATM card
die **Bar** bar (place)
das **Bargeld** n cash

der Baseball baseball (game)
der Basketball basketball (game)
die Batterie battery
die Bauchschmerzen stomachache
der Bauernhof *n* farm
der Baum tree
die Baumwolle cotton
die Beaufsichtigung supervision
die Bedienung service (in a restaurant)
beenden *v* exit (computer)
beginnen begin
behindert handicapped; **~engerecht** handicapped [disabled BE]-accessible
beige *adj* beige
die Beilage side order
das Bein leg
beinhalten include (tax)
die Bekleidung clothing
das Bekleidungsgeschäft clothing store
belasten *v* charge (credit card)
belästigen bother
die Belichtung exposure (film)
benachrichtigen notify
benutzen *v* use
der Benutzername username
das Benzin gas [petrol BE]
beobachten *v* watch

der Berater consultant
berauben rob
beraubt robbed
bereit ready
der Berg hill; **~** mountain
beschädigen *v* damage
beschädigt damaged
die Beschwerde complaint
die Beschwerden condition (medical)
der Besen broom
die Besichtigungstour sightseeing tour
besser better
bestätigen confirm
beste *adj* best
bestellen *v* order (restaurant)
besuchen *v* visit
die Besuchszeiten visiting hours
das Bett *n* bed
die Bettwäsche sheets
bewusstlos unconscious (condition)
bezahlen pay
die Beziehung relationship
der BH bra
der Bikini bikini
billig cheap
billiger cheaper
bitte please
die Blase bladder
blau *adj* blue
bleifrei unleaded (gas)
der Blinddarm appendix

(body part)
der Blindenhund guide dog
das Blitzlicht flashlight
die Blume n flower
die Bluse blouse
das Blut blood
der Blutdruck blood pressure
bluten bleed
der Blutstau congestion
das Boot boat
die Bordkarte boarding pass
**der botanische
Garten** botanical garden
der Boxkampf boxing match
die Bratpfanne frying pan
brauchen v need
braun adj brown
brechen v break
die Bremse brakes (car)
brennen v burn
der Brief letter
der Briefkasten mailbox
[postbox BE]
die Briefmarke n stamp
(postage)
die Brille glasses (optical)
bringen bring
britisch British
die Brosche brooch
die Brücke bridge
der Bruder brother
die Brust breast; ~ chest
~**schmerzen** chest pain
das Buch n book
die Bücherei library

der Buchladen bookstore
buchstabieren v spell
das Bügeleisen n iron
(clothes)
bügeln v iron
das Büro office
die Bürozeiten office hours
der Bus bus; ~**bahnhof** bus
station; ~**fahrschein** bus
ticket
die Bushaltestelle bus stop;
die Business-Class business
class
die Bustour bus tour

C

das Café cafe (place)
campen v camp
der Campingkocher camping
stove
der Campingplatz campsite
die Campingtoilette chemical
toilet
der Canyon canyon
das Casino casino
die CD CD
Celsius Celsius
das Check-in check-in
das Check-out check-out
chinesisch Chinese
der Club n club
der Computer computer
die Creme n cream (ointment)

D

danken thank
der Darm intestine
das (neuter) the
das Datum *n* date (calendar)
die Decke blanket
das Denkmal memorial (place)
das Deodorant deodorant
der the
das Deutsch German; **~land** Germany
der Diabetiker *n* diabetic
der Diamant diamond
die the
der Dieb thief; **~stahl** theft
diese this
der Diesel diesel
dieser this
dieses (neuter) this
digital digital
der Digitaldruck digital print
das Digitalfoto digital photo
die Digitalkamera digital camera
das Display *n* display
Dollar dollar (U.S.)
der Dolmetscher interpreter
das Doppelbett double bed
das Dorf village
dort there
der Dosenöffner can opener
draußen outside
dringend urgent

drucken *v* print
drücken *v* push
dunkel *adj* dark
der Durchfall diarrhea
durchreisen pass through
durstig thirsty
die Dusche *n* shower
das Dutzend dozen
die DVD DVD

E

echt real
die EC-Karte debit card
die Ecke *n* corner; **an der Ecke** on the corner
die Economy-Class economy class
die Ehefrau wife
der Ehemann husband
die Eile *n* rush
die Einbahnstraße one-way street
einbrechen *v* break in (burglary)
einchecken *v* check in
einführen *v* insert
der Eingang entrance
eingravieren engrave
der Einheimische *n* local (person)
einkaufen *v* shop
das Einkaufen shopping
der Einkaufskorb basket (grocery store)
der Einkaufswagen cart

[trolley BE] (grocery store)

das Einkaufszentrum shopping mall [centre BE]; ~ shopping area (town)

einlösen v cash (check)

einmal once

einpacken v wrap (parcel)

eins one

das Einschreiben registered mail

einsteigen v board (bus)

eintreten v enter

der Eintritt admission (fee)

der Einwegartikel n disposable

der Einweg-Rasierer disposable razor

einzahlen v deposit (money)

die Einzahlung n deposit (bank)

der Einzelabzug single print

das Einzelbett single bed

das Einzelzimmer single room

das Eis n ice; ~hockey ice hockey

der Ellenbogen elbow

die E-Mail n e-mail; ~-Adresse e-mail address; ~ senden v e-mail

empfehlen recommend

die Empfehlung recommendation

eng tight (fit)

englisch English

der Enkel grandchild

entleeren v empty

entschuldigen v excuse

entwerten v stamp (ticket)

entwickeln v develop (film)

epileptisch adj epileptic

erbrechen v vomit

erfahren adj experienced

erhalten receive

die Erkältung n cold (sickness)

erklären explain

erlauben allow

ernst serious

erreichen v reach

erschöpft exhausted

erstaunlich amazing

erste Klasse first class

erste adj first

erwärmen v warm (something)

essen eat

das Essen food

das Esszimmer dining room

die Etage floor [storey BE]

das E-Ticket e-ticket

etwas something; ~ mehr... some more...

der EU-Bürger EU resident

der Euro euro

die Exkursion excursion

der Experte n expert

der Express n express; ~bus express bus

extra extra; ~ groß extra large

F

die Fähre ferry
fahren v drive
die Fahrkarte ticket
der Fahrkartenschalter ticket office
das Fahrrad n bicycle
der Fahrradweg bike route
der Fahrstuhl elevator [lift BE]
die Fahrzeugregistrierung vehicle registration
die Familie family
die Farbe n color
das Fax n fax
faxen v fax
die Faxnummer fax number
der Fehler n mistake
fehlen be missing
der Urlaub vacation [holiday BE]
das Feinkostgeschäft delica-tessen
das Fenster window
der Fernseher television
das Festpreismenü fixed-price menu
die Festung fort
fettfrei fat free
das Feuer n fire
die Feuertür fire door
die Feuerwehr fire department
das Feuerzeug lighter
das Fieber fever

filetiert fileted (food)
der Film film (camera); ~ movie (cinema)
der Finger n finger
der Fingernagel fingernail
der Fitnessraum gym (workout)
die Flasche n bottle
der Flaschenöffner bottle opener
der Fleischer butcher
der Florist florist
der Flug flight
die Fluggesellschaft airline
der Flughafen airport
das Flugzeug airplane
der Fluss river
der Fön hair dryer
das Förderband conveyor belt
das Formular n form
fortgeschritten intermediate
das Foto photo
die Fotografie photography
fotografieren take a photo
die Fotokopie photocopy
die Frage n question
der Franzbranntwein rubbing alcohol [surgical spirit BE]
die Frau woman
freiberufliche Arbeit freelance work
frei adj free
das Fremdenverkehrsbüro tourist information office

die Freude pleasure
der Freund boyfriend; friend
die Freundin girlfriend; friend
frisch fresh
die Frischhaltefolie plastic wrap
der Friseur barber, hairstylist
der Friseursalon hair salon
die Frisur hairstyle
früh early
das Frühstück breakfast
der Führer guide
die Führerscheinnummer driver's license number
das Fundbüro lost-and-found
für for
der Fuß foot; **~ball** soccer
das Fußballspiel soccer match [football game BE]
der Fußgänger *n* pedestrian
das Fußgelenk *n* ankle
füttern *v* feed

G

die Gabel fork
der Gang aisle
die Garage garage
das Gate gate (airport)
das Gebäude building
geben *v* give
die Gebühr fee
der Geburtstag birthday
gefährlich dangerous
der Gefrierschrank freezer
das Gegenteil *n* opposite

gehen *v* go (somewhere)
gekocht stewed
das Gel gel (hair)
gelb *adj* yellow
das Gelbgold yellow gold
das Geld money
die Geldbörse wallet
der Geldschein *n* bill [note BE] (money)
das Gelenk joint (body part)
das Generikum generic drug [unbranded medication BE]
genießen *v* enjoy
das Gepäck baggage [luggage BE]
die Gepäckausgabe baggage claim
der Gepäckschein baggage [luggage BE] ticket
das Gepäckschließfach baggage [luggage BE] locker
der Gepäckwagen baggage [luggage BE] cart
geradeaus straight
gern geschehen you're welcome
das Geschäft business; **~** store **~sverzeichnis** store directory; **~szentrum** business center
das Geschenk gift
der Geschenkwarenladen gift shop
das Geschirr dishes (kitchen)
der Geschirrspüler

dishwasher
das Geschirrspülmittel
dishwashing liquid
geschlossen closed
**die Geschwindigkeitsüber-
schreitung** speeding
das Gesicht *n* face
gestern yesterday
gestohlen stolen
die Gesundheit health
das Getränk *n* drink
die Getränkekarte drink
menu
getrennt lebend separated
(person)
das Gewitter thunderstorm
gewürfelt diced (food)
das Gift *n* poison
der Gipfel peak (of a
mountain)
das Girokonto checking
[current BE] account
das Glas glass
gleich same
glücklich happy
die Glühbirne lightbulb
golden golden
der Golfplatz golf course
das Golfturnier golf
tournament
das Grad degree
(temperature)
das Gramm gram
grau *adj* gray
der Grill *n* barbecue

groß big; ~ large
großartig magnificent
das Großbritannien United
Kingdom (U.K.)
die Größe *n* size
die Großeltern grandparents
größer bigger; ~ larger
grün *adj* green
die Gruppe *n* group
gültig valid
der Gürtel belt
gut *adj* good; *adv* well;
~en Abend good evening;
~en Morgen good morning;
~en Tag good day
der Gynäkologe gynecologist

H

das Haar hair
die Haarbürste hairbrush
der Harfestiger mousse (hair)
der Haarschnitt haircut
das Haarspray hairspray
haben *v* have
halal halal
halb half; ~gar underdone;
die ~e Stunde half hour;
das ~e Kilo half-kilo
die Halbschuhe loafers
halbtags part-time
das Hallenbad indoor pool
Hallo hello
der Hals throat
die Halsschmerzen sore
throat

die **Haltestelle** *n* stop
der **Hammer** *n* hammer
die **Hand** *n* hand
das **Handgelenk** wrist
das **Handgepäck** hand luggage
die **Handtasche** purse [handbag BE]
das **Handtuch** towel
Handwäsche hand wash
das **Handy** cell [mobile BE] phone
hässlich ugly
die **Hauptattraktion** main attraction
das **Hauptgericht** main course
das **Haus** *n* house
das **Haushaltsgerät** utensil
die **Haushaltswaren** household goods
die **Haut** *n* skin
heiraten *v* marry
heiß hot (temperature);
~e **Quelle** hot spring;
~es **Wasser** hot water
heizen *v* heat
die **Heizung** heating
der **Hektar** hectare
helfen *v* help
der **Helm** helmet
das **Hemd** shirt
der **Herd** stove
das **Herz** heart

die **Herzkrankheit** heart condition
der **Heuschnupfen** hay fever
heute today; ~ **Abend** tonight
hier here
die **Hilfe** *n* help
die **Hin- und Rückfahrt** round-trip
Hinfahrt- one-way (ticket)
hinter behind (direction)
hoch high
das **Hockey** hockey
die **Höhle** *n* cave
hörgeschädigt hearing impaired
die **Hose** pants [trousers BE]
das **Hotel** hotel
hungrig hungry
husten *v* cough
der **Husten** *n* cough
der **Hut** hat

I

das **Ibuprofen** ibuprofen
die **Identifikation** identification
die **Impfung** vaccination
in in
infiziert infected
die **Information** information;
~ information desk
inländisch domestic
der **Inlandsflug** domestic flight
das **Insekt** bug

der Insektenschutz insect repellent
der Insektenstich insect bite
die Instant Message instant message
das Insulin insulin
interessant interesting
international international;
  der ~e Studentenausweis international student card;
  der ~e Flug international flight
das Internet internet;
  ~café internet cafe
der Internet-service internet service
irisch *adj* Irish
Irland Ireland
italienisch *adj* Italian

J

ja yes
die Jacke jacket
das Jahr year
japanisch Japanese
der Jazz jazz; **~club** jazz club
die Jeans jeans
der Jeansstoff denim
der Jet-ski jet ski
jetzt now
die Jugendherberge hostel;
  ~ youth hostel
jung *adj* young
der Junge boy
der Juwelier jeweler

K

das Kabarett cabaret
das Kaffeehaus coffee house
die Kalorie calorie
kalt *adj* cold (temperature);
  ~ cool (temperature)
die Kamera camera
die Kameratasche camera case
der Kamm *n* comb
das Kanada Canada
kanadisch *adj* Canadian
die Karaffe carafe
die Karte *n* card; **~** map
der Kassierer cashier
der Kater hangover (alcohol)
die Kathedrale cathedral
kaufen *v* buy
das Kaufhaus department store
der Kaugummi chewing gum
der Kellner waiter
die Kellnerin waitress
die Kette necklace
der Kiefer jaw
das Kilo kilo;
  ~gramm kilogram
der Kilometer kilometer
das Kind child
der Kinderarzt pediatrician
das Kinderbecken kiddie pool
das Kinderbett cot
die Kinderkarte children's

menu
die Kinderportion children's portion
der Kindersitz highchair
der Kinderstuhl child's seat;
der Kinderwagen stroller
das Kino movie theater
die Kirche church
das Kissen pillow
die Klarsichtfolie plastic wrap [cling film BE]
die Klasse class
die klassische Musik classical music
das Kleid n dress (clothing)
die Kleiderordnung dress code
klein small
der Kleintransporter van
die Klimaanlage air conditioning
die Klippe cliff
das Kloster monastery
das Knie n knee
der Knochen n bone
kochen v boil; ~ cook
das Kölnischwasser cologne
der Koffer suitcase
der Kollege colleague
kommen v come
die Konditorei pastry shop
das Kondom condom
die Konferenz conference
das Konferenzzimmer meeting room

der Kongressaal convention hall
die Konserve canned good
das Konsulat consulate
kontaktieren v contact
die Kontaktlinse contact lens
die Kontaktlinsenlösung contact lens solution
das Konto n account
das Konzert concert
die Konzerthalle concert hall
der Kopf n head (body part)
die Kopfhörer headphones
die Kopfschmerzen headache
der Korkenzieher corkscrew
koscher kosher
kosmetisch adj cosmetic;
~e **Gesichtsbehandlung** facial (treatment)
kosten v cost; ~ taste
krank ill; ~ sick
das Krankenhaus hospital
die Krankenschwester n nurse
der Krankenwagen ambulance
die Krawatte tie (clothing)
die Kreditkarte credit card
die Kreuzung intersection
das Kriegsdenkmal war memorial
das Kristall crystal (glass)
die Küche kitchen
die Küchenmaschine food

processor
der Kühlschrank refrigerator
die Kunst art
das Kupfer copper
kurz short; **~e Hose** shorts
kurzärmelig short-sleeved
kurzsichtig near- [short- BE] sighted
küssen *v* kiss

L

laktoseintolerant lactose intolerant
die Lampe *n* light (overhead)
die Landesvorwahl country code
landwirtschaftliches Erzeugnis produce
lang *adj* long; **~ärmlig** long-sleeved;
langsam slow; **~er** slower
langweilig boring
der Laufstall playpen
lauter louder
leben *v* live
das Lebensmittelgeschäft grocery store
die Leber liver (body part)
lecker delicious
das Leder leather
leicht easy
das Leinen linen
leise quiet
die Lektion lesson

letzte *adj* last
die Liebe *n* love
lieben *v* love (someone)
der Liegestuhl deck chair (ferry)
der Liftpass lift pass
die Linie line (train)
links left (direction)
die Linse lens
die Lippe lip
der Liter liter
Livemusik live music
locker loose (fit)
der Löffel *n* spoon
löschen *v* clear (on an ATM); **~** *v* delete (computer)
die Lotion lotion
die Luftpost *n* airmail
die Luftpumpe air pump
lufttrocknen *v* air dry
die Lunge lung

M

das Mädchen girl
das Magazin magazine
der Magen stomach
die Magenverstimmung upset stomach
die Mahlzeit meal
der Manager manager
die Maniküre *n* manicure
der Mann man (male)
der Mantel *n* coat
der Markt market

maschinentrocknen tumble dry

die Massage *n* massage

mechanisch *adj* mechanic

das Medikament medicine

die Medikamente medication

medium *adj* medium (meat)

das Meer sea

mehr more

die Mehrwertsteuer sales tax [VAT BE]

die Menstruationskrämpfe menstrual cramps

die Messe mass (church service)

messen *v* measure (someone)

das Messer knife

der Messbecher measuring cup

der Messlöffel measuring spoon

das Mietauto rental [hire BE] car

mieten *v* rent [hire BE]

die Mikrowelle *n* microwave

mild mild

die Mini-Bar mini-bar

die Minute minute

mit with; ~ **Bedienung** full-service

die Mitgliedskarte membership card

mitkommen *v* join

mitnehmen give somebody a lift (ride)

Mittag noon [midday BE]

das Mittagessen *n* lunch

Mitternacht midnight

der Mixer blender

die Mobilität mobility

mögen *v* like

der Monat month

die Monatsbinde sanitary napkin [pad BE]

der Mopp *n* mop

das Moped moped

morgen tomorrow

der Morgen morning

die Moschee mosque

der Moslem Muslim

das Motorboot motor boat

das Motorrad motorcycle

das Mountainbike mountain bike

müde tired

der Mund mouth

die Münze coin

das Münztelefon pay phone

das Museum museum

die Musik music

das Musikgeschäft music store

der Muskel muscle

die Mutter mother

N

nach after

der Nachmittag afternoon

nachprüfen *v* check (on something)

die Nachricht message
nachschneiden trim (haircut)
nächste adj next
die Nacht night
der Nachtclub nightclub
der Nacken neck
die Nagelfeile nail file
das Nagelstudio nail salon
nahe prep near
die Nähe vicinity;
  in der Nähe nearby
der Name n name
die Nase nose
die Nationalität nationality
das Naturreservat nature preserve
die Nebenstelle extension (phone)
die Nebenwirkung side effect
nehmen v take
nein no
Nichtraucher- non-smoking (area)
nichts nothing
niedrig low
die Niere kidney (body part)
der Norden n north
normal regular
der Notausgang emergency exit
der Notfall emergency
die Nummer n number
nur only; ~ just

O

obere adj upper
der Oberschenkel thigh
offen adj open
öffentlich adj public
öffnen v open
die Öffnungszeiten business hours
ohne without
das Ohr ear
die Ohrenschmerzen earache
der Ohrring earring
OK okay
das Öl n oil
die Oper opera
das Opernhaus opera house
der Optiker optician
orange adj orange (color)
das Orchester orchestra
die Ortsvorwahl area code
der Osten n east

P

packen v pack
die Packung carton;
  ~ packet
das Paket package
der Palast palace
paniert breaded
die Panne breakdown (car)
die Pantoffeln slippers
das Papier n paper
das Papierhandtuch paper towel

das **Paracetamol** acetaminophen [paracetamol BE]

das **Parfüm** n perfume

der **Park** n park

parken v park

das **Parkhaus** parking garage

der **Parkplatz** parking lot [car park BE]

die **Parkuhr** parking meter

das **Parlamentsgebäude** parliament building

das **Parterre** ground floor

der **Passagier** passenger

die **Passform** fit (clothing)

die **Passkontrolle** passport control

das **Passwort** password

die **Pediküre** pedicure

das **Penicillin** penicillin

der **Penis** penis

die **Pension** bed and breakfast

die **Periode** period (menstrual)

die **Perle** pearl

der **Pfad** path

die **Pferderennbahn** horsetrack

das **Pflaster** bandage

das **Pfund** n pound (weight)

das **Pfund** pound (British sterling)

die **Pille** Pill (birth control)

die **Piste** n trail [piste BE]

der **Pistenplan** trail [piste BE] map

die **Pizzeria** pizzeria

der **Plan** n schedule [timetable BE]; ~ map

planen v plan

das **Platin** platinum

der **Platte** flat tire

der **Platz** field (sports); ~ seat; ~ **am Gang** aisle seat

die **Plombe** filling (tooth)

der **Po** buttocks

die **Polizei** police

der **Polizeibericht** police report

das **Polizeirevier** police station

der **Pool** n pool

die **Popmusik** pop music

die **Portion** n portion

die **Post** mail [post BE]; ~ post office

die **Postkarte** postcard

der **Preis** price; ~ **pro Gedeck** cover charge

preisgünstig inexpensive

pro per; ~ **Nacht** per night; ~ **Stunde** per hour; ~ **Tag** per day; ~ **Woche** per week

das **Problem** problem

Prost! Cheers!

die **Prothese** denture

die **Puppe** doll

der **Pyjama** pajamas

Q

die Qualität *n* quality
die Quittung receipt

R

das R-Gespräch collect call [reverse charge call BE]
ein R-Gespräch führen *v* call collect [to reverse the charges BE]
der Rabatt discount
das Radfahren cycling
der Rap rap (music)
die Rasiercreme shaving cream
die Rasierklinge razor blade
der Rastplatz picnic area
das Rathaus town hall
der Rathausplatz town square
rauchen *v* smoke
Raucher- smoking (area)
die Rechnung bill [invoice BE] (of sale)
rechts right (direction)
das Recycling recycling
das Reformhaus health food store
der Regen *n* rain
die Regenjacke raincoat
der Regenschirm umbrella
der Regenwald rainforest
die Region region
regnerisch rainy

der Reifen tire [tyre BE]
reinigen *v* clean; **chemisch ~** dry clean
die Reinigung dry cleaner's
die Reinigungsmittel cleaning supplies
die Reise trip; **~** journey
das Reisebüro travel agency
der Reiseführer guide book
die Reisekrankheit motion sickness
der Reisepass passport
der Reisescheck traveler's check [cheque BE]
die Rennbahn racetrack
der Rentner senior citizen
reparieren *v* fix; **~** repair
reservieren *v* reserve
die Reservierung reservation
der Reservierungsschalter reservation desk
das Restaurant restaurant
der Rettungsschwimmer lifeguard
das Rezept prescription
die Rezeption reception
die Richtung direction
der Ring *n* ring
die Rippe rib (body part)
der Rock skirt
der Rollstuhl wheelchair
die Rollstuhlrampe wheelchair ramp
die Rolltreppe escalator

romantisch romantic
rosa *adj* pink
rot *adj* red
die Route route
der Rücken *n* back (body part)
die Rückenschmerzen backache
der Rucksack backpack
das Ruderboot rowboat
das Rugby rugby
die Ruine ruin

S

der Safe *n* safe (for valuables)
die Sandalen sandals
sauber *adj* clean
die Sauerstoffbehandlung oxygen treatment
die Saugglocke plunger
die Sauna sauna
der Scanner scanner
die Schachtel *n* pack; ~ **Zigaretten** pack of cigarettes
der Schal scarf
scharf hot (spicy); ~ sharp
das Schaufenster window case
der Scheck *n* check [cheque BE] (payment)
die Schere scissors
schicken send; **per Post ~** mail
das Schlachtfeld battleground

schlafen *v* sleep
die Schläfrigkeit drowsiness
der Schlafsack sleeping bag
die Schlafstörung insomnia
der Schlafwagen sleeper [sleeping BE] car
der Schläger racket (sports)
schlecht nauseous; ~ bad
der Schlepplift drag lift
schließen *v* close (a shop)
das Schließfach locker
das Schloss castle; ~ lock
die Schlucht ravine
der Schlüssel key; ~**ring** key ring
die Schlüsselkarte key card
der Schmerz pain; **Schmerzen haben** be in pain
der Schmuck jewelry
schmutzig dirty
der Schneeschuh snowshoe
schneiden *v* cut
schnell fast
der Schnellzug express train
der Schnitt *n* cut (injury)
der Schnuller pacifier [soother BE]
schön nice; ~ beautiful
schrecklich terrible
schreiben write
der Schrein shrine
der Schuh shoe
das Schuhgeschäft shoe store

die Schule school
die Schulter shoulder
die Schüssel bowl
schwanger pregnant
schwarz *adj* black
die Schwellung swelling
die Schwester sister
schwierig difficult
das Schwimmbad swimming pool
schwimmen *v* swim
die Schwimmweste life jacket
schwindelig dizzy
schwul *adj* gay
die Schwulenbar gay bar
der Schwulenclub gay club
der See lake
sehbehindert visually impaired
sehen *v* look; ~ see
die Sehenswürdigkeit attraction
die Seide silk
die Seife *n* soap
die Seilbahn cable car
sein *v* be
die Selbstbedienung self-service
selten rare
seltsam strange
das Seminar seminar
senden *v* send
die Serviette napkin
der Sessellift chair lift

sexuell übertragbare Krankheit sexually transmitted disease (STD)
das Shampoo *n* shampoo
sich scheiden lassen *v* divorce
sicher *adj* safe (protected)
die Sicherheit security
das Sieb colander
das Sightseeing sightseeing
das Silber *n* silver
sitzen *v* sit
der Ski *n* ski
Ski fahren *v* ski
der Skilift ski lift
der Slip briefs (clothing)
die SMS SMS;
eine SMS schicken *v* text (message)
das Snowboard *n* snowboard
die Socke sock
die Sonne *n* sun
der Sonnenbrand sunburn
die Sonnenbrille sunglasses
die Sonnencreme sunscreen
der Sonnenstich sunstroke
sonnig sunny
das Souvenir souvenir;
~geschäft souvenir store
das Sparkonto savings (account)
spät late (time)
der Spatel spatula
später later
spazieren gehen *v* walk

der **Spaziergang** n walk
die **Speicherkarte** memory card
speichern v save (computer)
die **Speisekarte** menu
der **Spezialist** specialist (doctor)
das **Spiel** game; ~ match
spielen v play
die **Spielhalle** arcade
der **Spielplatz** playground
das **Spielzeug** toy
der **Spielzeugladen** toy store
das **Spirituosengeschäft** liquor store [off-licence BE]
die **Spitze** lace (fabric)
der **Sport** sports
die **Sportmassage** sports massage
das **Sportgeschäft** sporting goods store
sprechen v speak
der **Springbrunnen** fountain
die **Spülung** conditioner (hair)
die **Stäbchen** chopsticks
das **Stadion** stadium
die **Stadt** city; ~ town
der **Stadtplan** town map
die **Stadtrundfahrt** sightseeing tour
das **Stadtzentrum** downtown area
die **Stange** carton (of cigarettes)

die **Statue** statue
der **Staubsauger** vacuum cleaner
das **Steakhouse** steakhouse
die **Steckdose** electric outlet
stehlen v steal
steil steep
das **Sterlingsilber** sterling silver
der **Stich** n sting
die **Stiefel** boots
der **Stift** pen
stillen breastfeed
die **Stöcke** poles (skiing)
stornieren v cancel
die **Strafe** n fine (fee for breaking law)
die **Strähnchen** highlights (hair)
der **Strand** beach
die **Straßenkarte** road map
der **Strom** electricity
die **Strumpfhose** pantyhose [tights BE]
das **Stück** n piece; ~ play (theater); ~ slice
der **Student** student
studieren v study
der **Stuhl** chair
der **Stuhlgang** stool (bowel movement)
die **Stunde** hour
der **Süden** n south
das **Super** super (fuel)
der **Supermarkt** supermarket

das Surfboard surfboard
das Surfbrett windsurfer (board)
süß cute; ~ sweet (taste)
die Süßigkeit candy [sweet BE]
das Sweatshirt sweatshirt
die Synagoge synagogue
synchronisiert dubbed

T

der Tabakhändler tobacconist
die Tablette tablet (medicine)
der Tag day
Tages- one-day (ticket)
das Tal valley
der Tampon tampon
tanken *v* fill (car)
die Tankstelle gas [petrol BE] station
der Tanzclub dance club
tanzen *v* dance
die Tasche bag; ~ pocket
die Tasse *n* cup
taub *adj* deaf
die Tauchausrüstung diving equipment
tauchen *v* dive
das Taxi taxi
das Team team
der Teelöffel teaspoon
der Teich pond
das Teil part (for car)
das Telefon *n* phone

das schnurlose Telefon wireless phone
der Telefonanruf phone call
die Telefonkarte phone card
die Telefonnummer phone number
der Teller plate
der Tempel temple (religious)
das Tennis tennis
der Termin appointment
der Terminal terminal (airport)
teuer expensive
der Text *n* text
das Theater theater
tief deep
die Tiefkühlkost frozen food
das Tier animal
der Tisch table
die Toilette restroom [toilet BE]
das Toilettenpapier toilet paper
der Topf *n* pot
die Töpferwaren pottery (pots)
die Tour *n* tour
der Tourist tourist
traditionell traditional
traurig sad
treffen meet
das Treffen meeting
trennen disconnect (computer)
die Treppe stairs

trinken *v* drink
das Trinkwasser drinking water
der Tropfen *n* drop (medicine)
das T-Shirt T-shirt
die Tür door
der Turm tower
die Turnschuhe sneaker

U

die U-Bahn subway [underground BE]
die U-Bahn-Haltestelle subway [underground BE] station
über *prep* over;
~ **Nacht** overnight;
~**fallen** *v* mug
die Übergröße plus size
überhitzen overheat (car)
übersetzen translate
überweisen *v* transfer (money)
um (die Ecke) around (the corner)
umändern alter
umarmen *v* hug
die Umkleidekabine fitting room
der Umschlag envelope
umsteigen *v* change (buses);
~ *v* transfer (change trains/flights)
umtauschen *v* exchange (money)

umwerfend stunning
unbeaufsichtigt unattended
der Unfall accident
die Universität university
die Unterhaltung entertainment (amusement)
die Unterhose underwear [underpants BE]
die Unterkunft accommodation
die Unterlegplane groundcloth
unterschreiben *v* sign
der Untertitel *n* subtitle
die Unterwäsche underwear
der Urin urine
der Urlaub vacation [BE holiday]

V

die Vagina vagina
vaginal vaginal; **die ~e Entzündung** vaginal infection
der Vater father
der V-Ausschnitt V-neck
der Veganer *n* vegan
der Vegetarier *n* vegetarian
der Ventilator fan (appliance)
verbieten *v* prohibit
verbinden *v* connect (internet)
die Verbindung connection
die Vereinigten Staaten United States (U.S.)
verfügbar available

vergewaltigen *v* rape
die Vergewaltigung *n* rape
der Vergnügungspark amusement park
verheiratet married
verkaufen *v* sell
verlangen *v* charge (cost)
verlieren *v* lose (something)
verlobt engaged
verloren lost
verschlucken *v* swallow
verschneit snowy
verschreiben *v* prescribe (medication)
versenden *v* ship
die Versicherung insurance
die Versicherungs-gesellschaft insurance company
die Versicherungskarte insurance card
die Verstauchung *n* sprain
verstehen understand
die Verstopfung constipation
verwitwet widowed
verzögern *v* delay
viel much; ~ a lot; **~en Dank** thank you; **wie ~** how much
violett *adj* purple
die Visitenkarte business card
das Visum visa
das Vitamin vitamin
die Vitrine display case

der Vogel bird
die Volksmusik folk music
das Volleyballspiel volleyball game
Vollzeit- full-time
vor before; **Viertel ~ vier** a quarter to four
die Vorfahrt right of way
die Vorhersage *n* forecast
die Vorspeise appetizer [starter BE]
vorstellen *v* introduce (person)
vorübergehend temporary

W

wählen *v* dial
während during
die Währung currency
der Währungsumtausch currency exchange
der Wald forest
die Wanderroute walking route
die Wanderschuhe hiking boots
die Wanduhr wall clock
wann when (time)
die Ware *n* good; ~ product
die Waren goods
warm *adj* warm (temperature)
warten wait
der Warteraum waiting room
die Wartezeit *n* waiting period

was what
das Waschbecken n sink
die Wäscherei laundry (facility)
der Wäscheservice laundry service
die Waschmaschine washing machine
waschmaschinenfest machine washable
das Waschmittel detergent
der Waschsalon laundromat [launderette BE]
der Wasserfall waterfall
die Wasserski water skis
das Wechselgeld n change (money)
der Wechselkurs exchange rate
wechseln v change
die Wechselstube currency exchange office
wecken v wake
der Weckruf wake-up call
weich soft
das Weingut vineyard
die Weinkarte wine list
weiß adj white
das Weißgold white gold
weit adv far (distance); ~ adj loose (fit)
weitsichtig far [long BE]-sighted
das Wellness-Center spa
wenig adj little (not much)

weniger less
wer who
der Wert value
wertvoll valuable
der Westen n west
das Wetter weather
wickeln v change (baby)
wie how; ~ **viel** how much
wiederholen repeat
willkommen adj welcome
die Windel diaper [nappy BE]
die Wirbelsäule spine (body part)
wireless wireless
wo where
die Woche week
das Wochenende weekend
wöchentlich weekly
der Wohnwagen mobile home
die Wolle wool
wunder schön beautiful
die Wüste n desert

Z

der Zahn tooth
der Zahnarzt dentist
die Zahnpaste toothpaste
der Zeh n toe
der Zehennagel toenail
das Zeichen symbol (keyboard)
zeigen v show (somebody something)
die Zeit time

der Zeitraum period (of time)
die Zeitung newspaper
der Zeitungskiosk newsstand
das Zelt tent
der Zelthering tent peg
die Zeltstange tent pole
der Zentimeter centimeter
zerbrochen broken
(smashed)
das Zertifikat certificate
ziehen *v* extract (tooth);
~ *v* pull (door sign)
die Zigarette cigarette
die Zigarre cigar
das Zimmer room

der Zimmerschlüssel room
key
der Zimmerservice room
service
das Zinn pewter
der Zoll customs; ~ duty
(tax)
zollfrei duty-free
der Zoo zoo
zu *adv* too; ~ *prep* to
der Zug train
die Zunge tongue
zurückgeben *v* return
(something)
der Zutritt *n* access